Event-Triggered and Time-Triggered Control Paradigms

REAL-TIME SYSTEMS SERIES

Consulting Editor: **John A. Stankovic,** *University of Virginia*

Event-Triggered and Time-Triggered Control Paradigms

Roman Obermaisser

Vienna University of Technology
Vienna, Austria

Foreword by Hermann Kopetz

Springer

ISBN: 978-1-4419-3569-4
eBook ISBN: 978-0-387-23044-3
eBook ISBN: 0-387-23044-0

Visit Springer's eBookstore at: http://www.ebooks.kluweronline.com
and the Springer Global Website Online at: http://www.springeronline.com

Contents

Foreword

More than twenty-five generations of semiconductor chips have followed Moore's law (which states that the number of devices that can be placed on a single die doubles about every two years). Up to today, this has led to the development of Systems-on-a-Chip (SoCs) with more than one hundred million devices. According to industry forecasts, this increase in device density will continue at least until the end of this decade, resulting in SoCs with about a billion devices. Despite this tremendous increase in the number of functions per chip, the reliability of a chip with respect to permanent hardware faults has remained more or less the same over the years – a mean-time-to-fail (MTTF) of about one thousand years. This implies that in the past decades the reliability per function has increased as dramatically as the increase in the number of devices per chip.

It is an architectural challenge to exploit these technological advances in function dependability in order to increase the dependability of services at the system level, particularly in the field of safety-critical control applications. In these application a service reliability at the system level of better than 100 000 years must be achieved. Despite the observed remarkable level of reliability of state-of-the-art semiconductor chips, such a high system reliability can only be achieved by the implementation of fault-tolerance. Fault tolerance can be realized by replicating functions at independent fault-containment units (FCU), i.e. on independent SoCs and matching the independently computed outputs by a (replicated) voter, outvoting the result of a faulty component. In order to achieve the necessary level of independence of the FCUs – also with respect to spatial proximity faults – a physically distributed architecture is an absolute requirement. The physical distribution of nodes that is needed in order to assure independent failures of FCUs is thus dictated by dependability concerns and will not be affected by a further increase of the functional capabilities of the ever more powerful SoCs.

Today's state of the art distributed systems, e.g., in the automotive industry, are federated. In a federated architecture every function is hosted at a dedicated node computer. The communication to the other nodes of a given distributed application subsystem is realized by a dedicated network. This leads to a high number of system nodes – close to 100 in current premium cars – and a large number of cables and connector points. The main advantages of a federated architecture are the strong fault isolation properties and the physically constrained possibilities of error propagation. Other advantages relate to the clear management responsibility for a distributed application subsystem and the possibility to protect the intellectual property of the software provider.

A significant reduction in the number of node computers and the number of cables could be achieved if a single SoC could host several functions of different criticality and if many different virtual communication channels with known temporal properties could share a single physical wire. This reduction in the number of nodes and cabling points leads already to a marked improvement in the hardware dependability. A further dependability improvement can be realized if the integrated architecture provides structural support for the implementation of transparent fault tolerance by replicating functions on different SoCs and voting on the results.

However, even a slight interference between the diverse software functions implemented within a multi-criticality node could cancel out all those stipulated advantages. An integrated architecture must thus contain effective mechanisms for fault isolation, error containment and diagnosis in order not to lose the advantages of the federated approach.

The first part of this very readable book by Roman Obermaisser gives an excellent survey about existing architectures for safety-critical applications and discusses the issues that must be considered when moving from a federated to an integrated architecture. It then focuses on one key topic, the amalgamation of the event-triggered and the time-triggered control paradigm into a coherent integrated architecture. The architecture provides for the integration of independent distributed application subsystems by introducing multi-criticality nodes and virtual networks of known temporal properties. In order to reduce the complexity of application software development, a virtual network with a single name-space can span multiple physical networks and hide the physical gateways between these networks. The subjects of fault isolation, error containment and diagnosis are treated with utmost care in order to maintain the advantages of the federated approach and to avoid any increase in application software complexity when moving to an integrated environment. The architecture supports the migration of legacy software by emulating widely used communication interfaces, such as the CAN interface in both, the value and the temporal domain. The architecture has been implemented on a distributed TTP/C/LINUX prototype. The feasibility and the tangible advantages of this new architecture have been demonstrated on practical examples taken from the automotive industry. I am sure that the interested reader will gain deep insights into the architecture and design of integrated embedded systems, both at the conceptual and at the practical level.

Hermann Kopetz
Vienna University of Technology

Preface

The shift from federated to integrated systems is a hot topic in many industries, such as the automotive and the avionic domain. In a federated system, each major function (e.g., autopilot in avionic system or brake-by-wire in automotive system) has its own dedicated computer system with internal redundancy, while an integrated system is characterized by the integration of multiple functions within a single distributed computer system. Federated systems have been preferred for ultra-dependable applications due to the natural separation of application functions, thus minimizing interactions and dependencies between the various autonomous computer systems. The ability to reason about the behaviour of an application function in isolation helps in controlling overall complexity. However, integrated systems promise massive cost savings through the reduction of resource duplication. In addition, integrated systems permit an optimal interplay of application functions, reliability improvements with respect to wiring and connectors, and overcome limitations for spare components and redundancy management. An ideal future system architecture combines the complexity management advantages of the federated approach, but also realizes the functional integration and hardware efficiency benefits of an integrated system.

The major contribution of this work is the introduction of a generic system architecture for integrated systems that preserves the advantages of the federated system approach. This goal is reached by the provision of error containment mechanisms through generic architectural services. In addition, the integrated architecture supports different paradigms of temporal control. It has been recognized that communication protocols fall into two general categories with corresponding strengths and deficiencies: event-triggered and time-triggered control. Event-triggered protocols (e.g., TCP/IP, CAN, Ethernet, ARINC629) offer flexibility and resource efficiency. Time-triggered protocols (e.g., TTP, SafeBus, FlexRay, Spider) excel with respect to predictability, composability, error detection and error containment. Through the support for both time-triggered and event-triggered communication activities, the integrated architecture is suitable for mixed-criticality and legacy integration. Safety-critical time-triggered applications coexist with event-triggered legacy applications and newly developed, non-critical event-triggered applications.

Our starting-point is a time-triggered architecture, for which we assume a set of four fundamental, basic services: a predictable, fault-tolerant time-triggered transport service, clock synchronization, error containment, and a membership service. On top of these basic services, we construct higher-level services for handling imprecise temporal specifications in the event-triggered subsystem: an event-triggered transport service, gateway services, membership information for event-triggered application tasks, and additional error containment mechanisms for preventing propagation of software faults. Furthermore, this book devises a solution for the reuse of event-triggered legacy applications in the proposed system architecture. We describe a generic model for the establishment of existing event-triggered communication protocols on top of basic, time-triggered architectural services. This approach supports a gradual evolution of systems and improves event-triggered communication services through a reliable underlying time-triggered subsystem.

The CAN emulation in the Time-Triggered Architecture is an application of the generic system architecture for the integration of event-triggered and time-triggered services. The CAN emulation is of high industrial relevance for the automotive domain, since the CAN protocol is widely used in present day automotive networks for powertrain and body/comfort functions. Despite the use of time-triggered architectures in future by-wire cars, CAN is likely to remain as a communication protocol for non-safety critical functions due to the higher flexibility and average performance. Even for safety-related functions, CAN-based legacy applications will not be replaced instantly.

This work is a revised version of my dissertation, which was carried out at the Vienna University of Technology during 2002–2003. This work has been supported, in part, by the NextTTA Research Project 'High-Confidence Architecture for Distributed Control Applications' (IST-2001-32111).

The completion of this book would not have been possible without the continuous support from various people and institutions. Above all, I would like to thank my thesis advisor Prof. Hermann Kopetz for his valuable support and numerous fruitful discussions. I have been honored to share his long experience in the field of distributed real-time systems. I would also like to thank him for providing the foreword to this book. Furthermore, my gratitude goes to my secondary advisor Prof. Wolfgang Kastner for interesting discussions and helpful suggestions. I would also like to thank Jack Stankovic, who provided suggestions for my thesis and established the contacts with Kluwer Academic Publishers.

Thanks also to all my colleagues from the department of Technische Informatik at the Vienna University of Technology, who have given me their support by proofreading as well as a very pleasant working environment. I would particularly like to express my thanks and appreciation to Philipp Peti for his close cooperation and friendship and for his valuable inputs.

Comments and suggestions concerning this book will be welcomed and can be sent to me by e-mail at ro@vmars.tuwien.ac.at.

ROMAN OBERMAISSER

Chapter 1

INTRODUCTION

Advances in computer and communication technologies have made it feasible to extend the application of embedded computer systems to more and more critical applications, such as automotive and avionic systems. Due to the many different and, partially, contradicting requirements, there exists no single model for building systems that interact with a physical environment. Well-known trade-offs are predictability versus flexibility, and resource adequacy versus best-effort strategies [Kopetz, 1997]. Thus, the chosen system model depends heavily on the requirements of the application.

For example, in safety-critical real-time control applications, such as X-by-wire systems in the automotive or avionic domain, a system's inability to provide its specified services can result in a catastrophe involving endangerment of lives and/or financial loss an order of magnitude higher than the overall cost of the system. These hard real-time systems must be designed according to the resource adequacy policy by providing sufficient computing resources to handle the specified worst-case load and fault scenarios.

At present, two different paradigms are prevalent in the design of real-time architectures. In *event-triggered architectures* the system activities, such as sending a message or starting computational activities, are triggered by the occurrence of events in the environment or the computer system. In *time-triggered architectures,* activities are triggered by the progression of global time. The major contrast between event-triggered and time-triggered approaches lies in the location of control. Time-triggered systems exhibit autonomous control and interact with the environment according to an internal predefined schedule, whereas event-triggered systems are under the control of the environment and must respond to stimuli as they occur.

The time-triggered approach is generally preferred for safety-critical systems [Kopetz, 1995b; Rushby, 2001a]. For example, in the automotive industry a time-triggered architecture will provide the ability to handle the communication needs of by-wire cars [Bretz, 2001]. In addition to hard real-time performance, time-triggered architectures help in managing the complexity of fault-tolerance and corresponding formal dependability models, as required for the establishment of ultra-high reliability [Suri et al., 1995] (failure rates in the order of 10^{-9} failures/hour). The predetermined points in time of the periodic message transmissions allow error detection and establishing of membership information. Redundancy can be established transparently to applications [Bauer and Kopetz, 2000], i.e. without any modification of the function and timing of application systems. A time-triggered system also supports replica determinism [Poledna, 1995], which is essential for establishing fault-tolerance through active redundancy. Furthermore, time-triggered systems support temporal composability [Kopetz and Obermaisser, 2002] via a precise specification of the interfaces between subsystems, both in the value and time domain. The communication controller in a time-triggered system decides autonomously when a message is transmitted. The communication network interface is a temporal firewall which isolates the temporal behavior of the host and the rest of the system.

In non safety-critical (soft real-time) applications, however, the event-triggered control paradigm may be preferred due to higher flexibility and resource efficiency. Event-triggered architectures support dynamic resource allocation strategies and resource sharing. In event-triggered systems the provision of resources can be biased towards average demands, thus allowing timing failures to occur during worst-case scenarios in favor of more cost-effective solutions. If the correlation between the resource usages of different applications is known, resources can be multiplexed between different applications while providing probabilistic guarantees for communication latencies and sufficiency of buffering capacities.

In addition to the classification of distributed real-time systems into event-triggered and time-triggered systems according to the employed paradigm of control, one can perform a differentiation of computer systems according to the level of integration into *federated* and *integrated systems*. These two classes of systems differ in the allocation of functions to the available computer systems. In a federated system, every major subsystem is implemented on its own dedicated distributed computer system. Subsystems are interconnected by gateways in order to realize a limited level of coordination in the interaction with the controlled object. An integrated system, on the other hand, is characterized by the integration of multiple application subsystems within a single distributed computer system. An *integrated architecture* provides a framework for the construction of such an integrated system. By restoring the level of fault isolation and error containment of a federated system, an integrated architecture promises a better coordination of control functions, a significant reduction of hardware resources and an overall improvement in the dependability.

1.1 Goal of this book

Many computer systems in the avionics and automotive domain are mixed-criticality systems. For example, in-vehicle electronics in the automotive industry involve numerous functions with different criticality levels. The spectrum starts at control applications for comfort electronics like seat and window movement controls that are non safety-critical. Modern cars also contain safety-related functions such as engine management and anti-lock braking. X-by-wire systems, which use electronics for control without mechanical or hydraulic backup systems impose the highest reliability requirements in automotive and avionic applications.

The objective of this book is the development of an integrated system architecture for the coexistence of subsystems with different degrees of synchrony and criticality. A single distributed computing platform serves as a shared resource for different functions and supports both the event-triggered and time-triggered control paradigms.

The primary goal of the integrated system architecture is the support for ultra-dependable hard real-time systems through a stable set of architectural services. In particular, error containment mechanisms must ensure the protection of safety-critical functions from the effects of misbehaving functions of lower levels of criticality. Otherwise, the potential for error propagation from a non-critical function to a function of higher criticality would elevate the criticality of the first one to the level of the second one.

A secondary goal of the integrated architecture is the establishment of generic higher-level services tailored to non safety-critical applications. In these applications, emphasis lies on low-cost, flexibility and resource efficiency. For economic reasons, non safety-critical applications can be designed non resource-adequately. Furthermore, incomplete knowledge about computational latencies and input load can lead to imprecise temporal specifications. We aim at providing higher-level services in an integrated architecture for handling these imprecise temporal specifications and the resulting occasional timing failures. These services include a best-effort communication service, gateway services, membership information, and additional error containment mechanisms for preventing propagation of software faults.

This book devises solutions for the integration of the event-triggered and time-triggered communication paradigms in a proposed system architecture by layering event-triggered communication on top of a time-triggered communication service. The layering of event-triggered on top of time-triggered services promises to minimize the effects of the best-effort communication service on the basic transport service. Furthermore, the event-triggered protocol can benefit from the fault-tolerance mechanisms of the underlying time-triggered basic transport protocol. The event-triggered and time-triggered communication services, as well as the corresponding applications employ a single fault-tolerant distributed computer system. Event-triggered and time-triggered functions share common computing resources, instead of using dedicated physical networks and node computers.

The proposed integrated system architecture will result in quantifiable cost reductions in the development and deployment of embedded systems in the areas of system hardware cost and maintenance. The integration of event-triggered and time-triggered communication services on top of a single physical network reduces physical wiring. In addition, the sharing of components via encapsulated execution environments for applications of different levels of criticality leads to a reduction of the overall number of components. In order to quantify these savings, we will estimate the implications of the sharing of physical networks and node computers onto the required number of hardware units on-board a high-end car.

Let us assume that the multiplexing of component and network resources will result in a reduction of 20% of the hardware units and a corresponding reduction in the number of wiring points of a car. On the other side, the new hardware units will be more powerful and may thus cost more. If we consider a typical high-end distributed system on board a car with 50 components, each node costing on average about € 35 and 1000 wires, each wire costing about € 0.5, then the total hardware cost of such a system is about € 2250. If an integrated system is deployed, the number of components will be reduced to 40 components of € 40 each (increase of the node cost by € 5), and the number of wires to 800. The total hardware cost will thus be reduced to € 2000 or € 250 per system. A hardware cost reduction of about 10% can thus be realized. The induced savings in the hardware domain during the production of 100 000 cars amount then to about € 25 Mio.

For estimating the implications with respect to maintenance cost, let us assume that the cost of maintenance of an electronic system onboard a car is about € 300 per car over the lifetime of a car. By reducing the number of components by 20% and the number of wiring points by 20%, a reduction of the maintenance cost by 20% can be expected. The induced savings in the maintenance domain in 100 000 cars amount then to about € 6 Mio, not considering the image gain of the manufacturer due to the improved dependability of its product.

A further economically relevant goal of this book is the reuse of event-triggered legacy applications. At present, the CAN protocol is widely used in automotive networks. In modern cars CAN is employed for powertrain, and body/comfort networks [Leen et al., 1999]. Body and comfort networks control seat and window movement and other non-critical user interfaces. Powertrain networks interconnect electronic control units (ECUs) for engine management, anti-locking braking (ABS), electronic stability programs (ESP) [Bosch, 1998], transmission control, and cruise control.

Driven by the introduction of X-by-wire functionality, future generations of cars will contain time-triggered networks [Bretz, 2001]. However, due to the higher flexibility and average performance, an event-triggered CAN communication service is likely to remain as the communication infrastructure for non safety-critical applications in cars. Even for safety-related functions, time-triggered solutions will not replace CAN-based solutions instantly. In this context, the CAN emulation in a time-triggered environment enables the integration of applications for which a CAN communication service is preferable, as well as the integration of CAN legacy applications into a time-triggered computing platform. By providing CAN execution environments within nodes of a time-triggered system in combination with CAN overlay networks, there is the potential for a significant reduction in the number of ECUs and wiring. In addition to lower cost, this strategy increases reliability as wiring and connectors are currently a prevalent source of faults in the automotive area [Swingler and McBride, 1999].

We will demonstrate the utility of the concepts for the integration of event-triggered and time-triggered services by instantiating the proposed integrated system architecture for employing a CAN communication service on top of the Time-Triggered Architecture [Kopetz and Bauer, 2003]. This instantiation provides an authentic CAN communication service, as required for the integration of CAN-based legacy applications. We identify and establish significant properties of a conventional CAN network (message ordering, message permanence, message cancelability, transmission latencies). We further show that this CAN emulation solves prevalent problems of the CAN protocol [Bosch, 1991] (e.g., fault-tolerant atomic broadcast, inaccessibility). An implementation of this CAN emulation model serves as a proof-of-concept of our integrated system architecture.

1.2 Overview

The book is organized as follows: Chapter 2 introduces the basic terms and concepts that are used throughout this book. The first part of this chapter describes distributed real-time systems and concepts of dependability. Afterwards, we give a brief overview of different synchrony models and present the event-triggered and time-triggered communication system paradigms. In addition, we map these control paradigms to prevalent models of computation.

Chapter 3 focuses on the requirement of an integrated system architecture for ultra-dependable real-time systems. We discuss four integration directions, with emphasis on the necessary architectural services. We summarize the basic services of an integrated architecture for ultra-dependable systems and outline higher-level services for easing application development.

Chapter 4 presents the integrated system architecture for the event-triggered and time-triggered control paradigms. We relate this architecture to the well-studied models of synchronous and asynchronous systems. Subsequently, we specify the basic and higher-level services of the integrated system architecture. The second part of this chapter defines the underlying fault hypothesis and provides information about the construction of error detection and error containment mechanisms.

Chapter 5 performs an instantiation of the integrated system architecture for providing CAN communication services on top of the Time-Triggered Architecture.

We first give a brief introduction about the Time-Triggered Architecture and the CAN protocol. We identify significant properties of CAN and present a solution for emulated CAN communication services. The chapter ends with an overview of a prototype implementation.

Chapter 6 demonstrates the CAN emulation's ability to handle the communication needs of newly developed CAN applications and CAN-based legacy applications. The analysis occurs through a comparison of measurement results from the prototype implementation with simulations of a conventional CAN network. In particular, this chapter discusses the improvements of the CAN emulation in relation to a physical CAN network.

Finally, the book ends with a conclusion in chapter 7 summarizing the key results of the presented work.

Chapter 2

BASIC CONCEPTS AND RELATED WORK

This chapter presents the basic concepts and terminology used in this book and gives an overview of system architectures for ultra-dependable, distributed real-time systems. Consequently, the first part of this chapter starts with an overview of distributed real-time systems and fundamental concepts of dependability in distributed real-time systems. We also present synchrony models that have been the focus of intensive theoretical studies. The second part describes event-triggered and time-triggered systems and relates these control paradigms to prevalent computational models. This chapter ends with a discussion of distributed system architectures for ultra-dependable systems and relates each architecture to the event-triggered and time-triggered computational models.

2.1   Distributed Real-Time Systems

A real-time computer system is a computer system in which correctness of the system behavior depends not only on the logical results of the computations, but also on the physical instants at which these results are produced [Kopetz, 1997, p. 2]. The real-time computer system and the enclosing environment form a larger system called the *real-time system.* The real-time computer system must react to stimuli from the controlled object in the environment within time intervals specified via *deadlines.* If a result has utility even after the deadline has passed, the deadline is classified as *soft.* Deadlines are called *hard deadlines,* if catastrophic consequences can result from missing a deadline. A real-time computer system that must meet at least one hard deadline is called a *hard real-time computer system* or a *safety-critical real-time computer system* [Kopetz, 1997]. In a soft real-time computer system no catastrophic consequences arise through deadline violations.

If the real-time computer system is distributed, it consists of a set of nodes interconnected by a real-time communication system. Each node can be partitioned into at least two subsystems, a communication controller and a host computer. The interface between the communication controller and the host computer is called the *communication network interface.* The set of communication controllers and the common communication network form the *communication system.* The purpose of the communication system is the transport of messages from the CNI of a sender to the CNIs of the receivers.

Component and Component Interfaces

In many engineering disciplines, the term component refers to a building block in the design of a larger system. In the context of distributed embedded real-time systems, a complete node seems to be the best choice for a component [Kopetz, 1998a], since the component-behavior can then be specified in the domains of value and time. Thus, a component is considered to be a self-contained computational element with its own hardware (processor, memory, communication interface, and interface to the controlled object) and software (application programs, operating system). The integration of components into a larger system is realized via a communication service that enables components to exchange messages across their linking interfaces (LIFs) [Kopetz and Suri, 2003]. The linking interface reduces a component functional and temporal description of those services that are required for the integration. The internal structure of the component is encapsulated and hidden from the user.

Linking interfaces are specified through an operational and a meta-level specification. The operational specification consists of the syntactic specification and the temporal specification. The syntactic specification defines the structure and the name of the exchanged messages. The temporal specification defines the temporal sequence of message exchanges. The meta-level specification defines the semantic by assigning meaning to information.

The LIF can be decomposed into a service requesting linking interface (SRLIF) and a service providing linking interface (SPLIF). A component offers its services to its environment via the SPLIF. The SRLIF enables a component to exploit services provided by other components. A component can depend on these services for being able to offer its own services via the SPLIF.

Concepts of Time, State, and Event

The concepts of time and state are fundamental in computer science. A common concept of time is a prerequisite for the consistent specification of time-out values, which are required in many communication protocols. In real-time systems, the validity of real-time information depends on the progression of physical time. For example, it makes little sense to use the measured angular position of a crankshaft in an automotive engine, if the precise instant when this position was measured is not recorded as part of the measurement [Jones et al., 2002]. In dependable systems, concepts of time and state are necessary in the construction of mechanisms for the detection and handling of failures. The detection of even the simplest external failure mode of a component, a crash failure [Laprie, 1992], depends on error detection in the temporal domain. The masking of faults by voting requires a consistent notion of state in replicas.

Concept of Time

In the context of real-time systems a time model based on Newtonian absolute time seems to be the best choice. In this model, the continuum of real-time can be modeled by a directed timeline consisting of an infinite set of instants [Whitrow, 1990]. In a distributed computer system, nodes capture the progression of time with physical clocks containing a counter and an oscillation mechanism. A physical clock partitions the time line into a sequence of nearly equally spaced intervals, called the micro granules of the clock, which are bounded by special periodic events, the ticks of the clock. An observer can record the current granule of the clock to establish the *timestamp* of an occurrence.

Since any two physical clocks will employ slightly different oscillators, the time-references generated by two clocks will drift apart. Clock synchronization is concerned with bringing the time of clocks in a distributed system into close relation with respect to each other. A measure for the quality of clock synchronization is the precision, which is defined as the maximum offset between any two clocks during an interval of interest. By performing clock synchronization in an ensemble of local clocks, each node can construct a local implementation of a global notion of time. The availability of such a synchronized global time [Lamport, 1984] simplifies the solution of agreement problems, because nodes can establish a consistent temporal order of events based on timestamps.

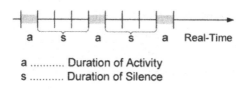

a .... Duration of Activity
s .... Duration of Silence

Figure 2.1.   Sparse Time Base

However, due to the synchronization and digitalization error it is impossible to establish the temporal order of occurrences based on their timestamp, if timestamps differ by only a single tick. A solution to this problem is the introduction of a *sparse time base* [Kopetz, 1992], where time is partitioned into an infinite sequence of alternating durations of activity and silence. The activity intervals establish a system-wide action lattice (see Figure 2.1). All occurrences within a specified duration of activity of the action lattice are considered to happen at the same time. If the lattice points of this action lattice are properly chosen, temporal order and simultaneity of occurrences can be realized based on timestamps without having to execute an agreement protocol.

While it is possible to restrict occurrences within the sphere of control of the computer system to these activity intervals, this is not possible for occurrences in the environment. Such occurrences happen on a dense time base and must be assigned to an interval of activity by an agreement protocol in order to get a system-wide consistent perception of when an occurrence happened in the environment.

Concept of State

The notion of state is fundamental for the investigation of complex systems. *State* is introduced in order to separate the past from the future. This book applies the definition of state by Mesarovic and Takahara [Mesarovic and Takahara, 1989]. This definition is based on the idea that *if one knows what state the system is in, he could with assurance ascertain what the output will be* [Mesarovic and Takahara, 1989, p. 45]. Hence, the state of a system embodies all past history of the given system and concentrates knowledge about occurrences of the past. In a deterministic system, future outputs solely depend on the current state and the future inputs.

Concept of Event

An *event* is a change of state, occurring at an instant [Nance, 1981]. An event is said to be determined, if the condition on event occurrence can be expressed strictly as a function of time. Otherwise, the event is contingent.

Concepts of Interface State and Function

The *interface state* [Jones et al., 2002] is part of the state of a component, namely the state as viewed from a particular interface. We define a *function* as an application specific input/output transformation that operates on the interface state of components. The function of a complete computer system is specified via the transformations of the state as viewed from the instrumentation interface. The function of a component are the transformations of the state as viewed from the linking interfaces.

Real-Time Entities, Objects, and Images

Real-time entities [Kopetz and Kim, 1990] are state variables of relevance. Real-time entities model the dynamics of a real-time application and change their state as time progresses. A real-time entity is located either in the environment or the controlling computer system. Every real-time entity is in the sphere of control of a subsystem that has the authority to set the value of the real-time entity. Outside its sphere of control, a real-time entity can only be observed.

A container within the computer system for holding a real-time entity is called *real-time object* [Kopetz and Kim, 1990]. In case of a distributed real-time object, every local site has its own replicated version of the real-time object. An example for such a distributed real-time object is global time, which provides the consistency constraint that at any point of real-time the clock value read by two nodes differs by at most one clock tick.

A *real-time image* is stored in a real-time object and provides the current picture of a real-time entity. The validity of a real-time image is time-dependent, which can be represented by the concept of *temporal accuracy* [Kopetz, 1997, p. 103]. A real-time image is temporally accurate, if its value is a member of the set of values that the real-time entity had in its recent history. The length of the recent history is denoted as *temporal accuracy interval*. The dynamics of a real-time entity determine the admissible temporal accuracy interval.

Types of Temporal Control Signals

A trigger is a control signal that initiates an action in the controlling computer system, like the execution of a task or the transmission of a message [Kopetz, 1993]. Depending on the source from which a trigger is derived, one can distinguish event triggers and time triggers.

Event Triggers

An *event trigger* is a control signal that is derived from an event, i.e. a state change in a real-time entity. The event can originate either from activities within the computer system (e.g., termination of a task) or from state changes in the natural environment (e.g., alarm condition indicated by a sensor element). In the latter case, the event trigger serves as a mechanism by which the environment delivers a service request to the controlling computer system. In general, such a service request will start a sequence of computational and communication activities.

Time Triggers

A *time trigger* is a control signal that is generated at a particular point in time of a synchronized global time base. Time triggers are solely derived from the progression of global time, which is a distributed real-time entity established by the clock synchronization service. The set of time triggers is a subset of the set of event triggers, since time triggers correspond to a particular class of events, namely changes in the state of global time. Time triggers are discriminated from other event triggers, since systems restricting control signals to time triggers offer properties that are desirable for distributed real-time systems. Among these properties are temporal predictability and composability [Kopetz, 1995b].

2.2   Concepts of Dependability

Dependability is the ability of a computing system to deliver services that can justifiably be trusted [Carter, 1982]. The service delivered by a system is its behavior as it is perceptible by another system (human or physical) interacting with the former [Laprie, 1992].

Dependability Threats – Failure, Error, Fault

A *failure* [Laprie, 1992] occurs when the delivered service deviates from fulfilling the functional specification. An *error* is that part of the system state which is liable to lead to a subsequent failure. A failure occurs when the error reaches the service interface. A *fault* is the adjudged or hypothesized cause of an error. As stated in [Avizienis et al., 2001], the concept of fault is introduced to stop recursion.

Due to the recursive definition of systems, a failure at a particular level of decomposition can be interpreted as a fault at the next upper level of decomposition, thereby leading to a hierarchical causal chain.

Fault Containment and Error Containment

A *fault containment region (FCR)* is defined as a subsystem that operates correctly regardless of any arbitrary logical or electrical fault outside the region [Lala and Harper, 1994]. The justification for building ultra-reliable systems from replicated resources rests on an assumption of failure independence among redundant units. For this reason the independence of FCRs is of critical importance [Butler et al., 1991]. The independence of FCRs can be compromised by shared physical resources (e.g., power supply, timing source), external faults (e.g., EMI, spatial proximity) and design.

Although an FCR can restrict the immediate the impact of a fault, fault effects manifested as erroneous data can propagate across FCR boundaries. For this reason the system must also provide error containment [Lala and Harper, 1994] to avoid error propagation by the flow of erroneous messages. The error detection mechanisms must be part of different FCRs than the message sender [Kopetz, 2003]. The *error containment region (ECR),* i.e. the set of FCRs that perform error containment, must consist of at least two independent FCRs. Otherwise, the error detection mechanism may be impacted by the same fault that caused the message failure.

Fault Hypothesis

The *fault hypothesis* specifies assumptions about the types of faults, the rate at which components fail and how components may fail [Powell, 1992]. The *assumption coverage* is the probability that these assumption hold in reality. Since fault-tolerance mechanisms of a system are based on these assumptions, the complete system can fail in case the assertions concerning faults, failure rates, and failure modes are violated.

Failure modes of components are defined through the effects as perceived by the service user, i.e. independently of the actual cause or rate of failures. Formally, a failure mode is defined in terms of an assertion on the sequence of value-time tuples that a failed or failing system is assumed to deliver [Powell, 1992]. Failure modes determine the degree of redundancy required to ensure correct error processing.

Based on the rigidity of assumptions, the following hierarchy of failures modes can be established [Cristian, 1991b]:

- **Fail-stop failures:** A fail-stop failures is defined as a component behavior, where the component does not produce any outputs. The component omits to produce output to subsequent inputs until it restarts. It is additionally assumed that all correct component detect the fail-stop failure.

- **Crash Failures:** A component suffering a crash failure does not produce any outputs. In contrast to fail-stop failures, a crash failure can remain undetected for correct components.

- **Omission Failures:** An omission failure occurs, if the sender component fails to send a message, or the receiver fails to receive a sent message. As a consequence, the receiver does not respond to an input. An omission failure can remain undetected for correct components.

- **Timing Failures:** The component does not meet its temporal specification. Outputs of a component are delivered too early or too late.

- **Byzantine or Arbitrary Failures:** There is no restriction on the effects a service user may perceive. Arbitrary failures include the forging of messages and "two-faced" component behaviors [Lamport et al., 1982].

2.3   Degrees of Synchrony

Existing models of distributed systems differ in their inherent notion of real-time. This is usually expressed in certain assumptions about process execution speeds and message delivery delays.

Asynchronous and Synchronous Systems

According to [Verissimo, 1997] the degree of synchrony of a system is defined by the system's compliance to five conditions:

S1   bounded and known processing speed

S2   bounded and known message delivery delay

S3   bounded and known local clock drift rate

S4   bounded and known load pattern

S5   bounded and known difference of local clocks

In *synchronous systems,* all five conditions are satisfied. In particular, there are known upper bounds of the durations of communication and processing activities.

The synchronous system model reduces the complexity of the design and implementation of dependable distributed applications, because non faulty processes can exploit the progression of time to predict each others' progress. For this reason, fault-tolerant systems for safety-critical control applications are usually based on the synchronous approach, although there are differences in the extent to which the basic mechanisms of the system guarantee the satisfaction of the synchrony assumption [Rushby, 1999b]. A high assumption coverage of the temporal bounds of the basic synchrony conditions is crucial, since synchronous systems are prone to incorrect behavior, if the implementation violates these timing constraints.

In the absence of such bounds, we speak of an *asynchronous system* [Fischer et al., 1985]. The asynchronous model contains the weakest assumptions, according to Schneider asynchrony is a "non-assumption" [Schneider, 1993]. Hence, an algorithm that works in the asynchronous model also works in all other models of synchrony. A fully asynchronous model has limitations restricting its usefulness in practical systems. Many problems of interest do not have deterministic solutions, as proven via impossibility results [Fischer et al., 1985; Lynch, 1989]. In particular, an asynchronous model does not allow timeliness specifications. In case of crash failures, it is impossible to guarantee to solve consensus within a bounded time. The main problem in the asynchronous model is the impossibility of distinguishing a slow processor from a failed processor.

Many existing systems are based on a model with an intermediate level of synchrony. For non safety-critical applications, probabilistic or partial satisfaction of synchrony assumption is often accepted for economic reasons. Examples of intermediate synchrony models are the timed asynchronous system model [Cristian and Fetzer, 1999], and the quasi-synchronous model [Verissimo and Almeida, 1995]. The *timed asynchronous system model* makes weak assumptions about the underlying infrastructure, more precisely it assumes no communication bounds and no global time. In a *quasi-synchronous* system a subset of the five synchrony conditions is satisfied only probabilistically, i.e. there is a known probability that an assumed bound does not hold.

Consensus Problem

Fundamental to cooperation in a distributed system is the ability of agreeing on a quantum of information in order to reach common decisions and to maintain the integrity of the system [Barborak et al., 1993, p. 171]. In the *consensus problem*, all correct processes propose a value and must reach a unanimous and irrevocable decision on some value that is related to the proposed values [Fischer, 1983]. The unanimity requirement ensures that in case all proposed values are identical, the consensus value is identical to this proposed value. Furthermore, the consensus value should depend on the initial values (non-triviality).

Two problems closely related to consensus are the *interactive consistency problem* [Pease et al., 1980] and the *byzantine generals problem* [Lamport et al., 1982]. The *interactive consistency problem* requires non-faulty processes to agree on a consistent vector called the consensus vector y. The ith element of y has to be the value proposed by process i, if i is non-faulty (validity). In the Byzantine Generals problem, a sender attempts to send a value to all other processors. All correct processes have to reach consensus on this value, if the sender is correct (strong generals problem). The weak generals problem only requires consensus, if no failure occurs during the protocol execution.

For the asynchronous system model, Fischer et. al proved that consensus is impossible, even if only one processor crashes during the protocol execution [Fischer et al., 1985]. This impossibility result is important because of the equivalence of the consensus problem with several other important problems. In [Fischer, 1983] the generals problem and interactive consistency are reduced to the consensus problem. The equivalence of the atomic broadcast problem and the consensus problem is shown in [Chandra and Toueg, 1996].

Failure Detectors

Inspired by the impossibility result of Fischer et al. [Fischer et al., 1985] research has been focused on the question how much synchrony is needed to achieve consensus in a distributed system [Dolev et al., 1987].

Chandra and Toueg [Chandra and Toueg, 1996] proposed an alternative approach to circumvent the impossibility result. In order to decide whether a process has actually crashed or is only very "slow", they augmented the asynchronous model of computation with *unreliable failure detectors,* i.e. an external failure detection mechanism that can erroneously indicate that a component has failed, only to correct the error at a later time. A distributed failure detector comprises a set of local failure detector modules. Each module maintains a list of processes which are currently suspected to have crashed and can add or remove processes from this list. Furthermore, the lists of suspects of two local failure detector modules can be different at any given time.

Failure detectors can be characterized according to the *completeness* and *accuracy* properties. Roughly speaking, completeness requires that every crashed process is eventually suspected and accuracy restricts the mistakes a failure detector can make.

In [Chandra et al., 1996] it has been shown that in order to solve *consensus,* any failure detector has to provide at least as much information as the *eventually weak failure detector* $\Diamond \mathcal{W}$. The definition of a class of failure detectors must be seen as a specification of the failure detection mechanism [Guerraoui and Schiper, 1997]. An optimal algorithm that implements the weakest failure detector is described in [Larrea et al., 2000].

2.4   Communication System Paradigms

Event-triggered and time-triggered communication systems are two different paradigms for the construction of the communication infrastructure of a distributed real-time system. The major difference between these paradigms lies in the location of control. Event-triggered communication systems are based on external control via event triggers. The decision when a message is to be transmitted is within the sphere of control of the application software in the host (see Figure 2.2). In a time-triggered communication system, the communication controller decides autonomously about the global points in time at which messages are transmitted. This autonomous control of a time-triggered communication system results from restricting temporal control signals to time triggers, which are independent of the state changes in the environment and the host computer.

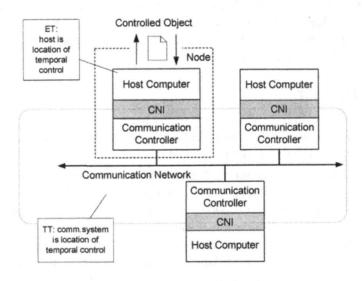

Figure 2.2.   Autonomous and External Control at the Communication System

This section compares event-triggered and time-triggered communication systems and presents distinctive features of the communication network interface in these two paradigms. Furthermore, we will discuss the data and control flow via the communication system and the requirements for an underlying transport protocol. The comparison of the two paradigms also includes a comparative evaluation of event-triggered and time-triggered communication systems.

Event-Triggered Communication Systems

An event-triggered communication system is designed for the sporadic exchange of event messages, combining event semantics with external control. At the sender side, these event messages are passed to the communication system via an explicit transmission request from the host application (external control) or as a result of the reception of a request message (e.g., client/server interaction). At the receiver side, the host application either fetches the incoming message from the communication system (polling for messages) or the communication system presses received messages into the host application (interrupt mechanism).

Supported Information Semantics

An event-triggered communication system can support the transmission of information with *event semantics* and/or *state semantics* [Kopetz, 1997]. Information with state semantics contains the absolute value of a real-time entity (e.g., temperature in the environment is 41 degrees Celsius). Since applications are often only interested in the most recent value of a real-time entity, state information allows the communication system to overwrite old state values with newer state values.

Information with event semantics relates to the occurrence of an event. Event information represents the change in value of a real-time entity associated with a particular event. Messages containing event information transport relative values (e.g., increase of the temperature in the environment by 2 degrees). In order to reconstruct the current state of a real-time entity from messages with event semantics, it is essential to process every message exactly-once. The loss of a single message with event information can affect state synchronization between a sender and a receiver.

Communication Network Interface

The Communication Network Interface (CNI) is the most important interface in a distributed real-time system [Kopetz, 1997], because it determines the abstraction a node forms in the context of a distributed real-time system.

We can classify event-triggered communication systems based on the direction of the control flow relative to the data flow at the CNI. Depending on the direction of the control flow relative to the data flow, one can distinguish an information push and an information pull behavior in the transfer of information between the host computer and the communication controller. In an *information push behavior* [DeLine, 1999], data and control flow have the same orientation, i.e. the information transfer occurs via the sender's request. An *information pull behavior* starts an information transfer via the receiver's request, data and control flow have complementary orientations.

- **Information Push for Information Flow from Host to Communication Controller:** The use of the information push principle for a host's message transmission requests is the prevalent type of control flow at the CNI in event-triggered communication systems. Thereby, the event-triggered system supports an event-based design, in which computational and communication activities a triggered by external stimuli and by the progression of computational activities.

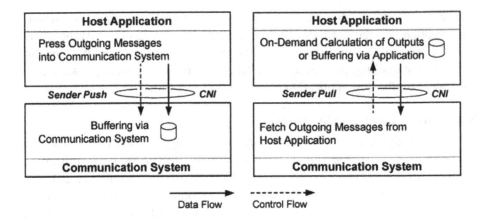

Figure 2.3.   Sender Push and Sender Pull at CNI for Outgoing Messages

As depicted in Figure 2.3, the application in the host computer presses messages into the communication system, e.g., requesting a message dissemination via a "send message" primitive. The information push principle for sending activities is therefore ideal for the host application, since the host application determines the points in time when data is transferred to the communication system.

This type of control also enables a generic buffer management for outgoing messages via the communication system. The need for buffering of messages arises, in case outgoing messages aggregate, e.g., due to the fact that the common network is occupied by other nodes or an application temporarily requests messages at a rate exceeding the available network bandwidth.

Although the buffer management functionality is application independent, the dimensioning of the intermediate structures at the communication system requires knowledge about interarrival times of messages from the host application in order to prevent buffer overflows. In case of an unrestricted rate of message transmission requests from the host computer, these intermediate data structures cannot be dimensioned and a potential overload of the communication system is inevitable.

- **Information Pull for Information Flow from Host to Communication Controller:** An information pull mechanism for outgoing messages at the CNI means that the communication system fetches outgoing message from the host application. An example for such a communication behavior occurs at the server side in a client/server interaction. A server object is a passive entity, which requires an external trigger (e.g., via the communication system) that results in computational activities and subsequently causes the dissemination of a response message.

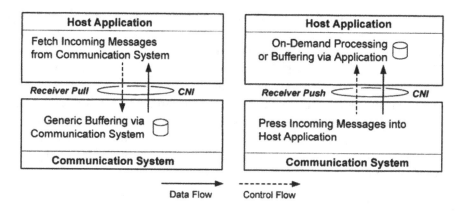

Figure 2.4. Receiver Push and Receiver Pull at CNI for Incoming Messages

Many programming languages for distributed systems provide support for such control patterns via synchronous message passing [Bal et al., 1989], i.e. a blocking send primitive that blocks until the communication partner has executed a corresponding receive statement.

- **Information Push for Information Flow from Communication Controller to Host:** An information push for message receptions means that the communication controller presses messages received via the network into the host application (see Figure 2.4). This control type for receptions represents the well-known interrupt mechanism. An information push CNI does not require restrictions of message interarrival times at the level of the communication system, since the communication system immediately forwards received messages to the host computer. The handling of the incoming message load is therefore shifted to the application software in the host computer. The main problem of this approach is the fact that the temporal behavior of the host application depends on the behavior of other applications that send messages.

- **Information Pull for Information Flow from Communication Controller to Host:** An information pull interface at the CNI requires the application in the host computer to fetch messages from the communication system. This is ideal for the application in the host computer, since it can determine the points in time when messages are retrieved and processed via the CNI.

The information pull mechanism prevents an interruption of application software through incoming messages. Incoming messages are buffered in intermediate datastructures and explicitly fetched by the application software. Similar to the information pull behavior for message transmissions, generic message buffering capabilities of the communication system are possible. Hence, incoming messages do not automatically lead to the consumption of computational resources.

The application can defer the processing of messages in case of high load. Nevertheless, the message buffering requires knowledge about the interarrival times of messages from the network and the service times of the application software. If for intervals of limited duration, the interarrival times of messages are smaller than the service times of messages at the host computer, the communication system can buffer messages in intermediate data structures. However, in case of unrestricted interarrival or service times, these intermediate data structures cannot be dimensioned and messages can be lost. The resulting message omission failures can affect state synchronization, if messages contain information with event semantics.

Transport Protocol

In an event-triggered communication system, the transport protocol must support the transmission of event messages with exactly-once delivery semantics in order to be able to maintain state synchronization. For preserving exactly-once delivery semantics in the presence of transient failures (e.g., omission or corruption of messages), many event-triggered transport protocols employ acknowledgments and timeouts in combination with unique identifiers or sequence numbers assigned to messages.

In a positive acknowledgment scheme, the receiver explicitly informs the sender about the successful reception of the message, which is identified in the corresponding acknowledgment message (e.g., via the sequence number). If the sender does not receive an acknowledgment message within a reasonable timeout, it will retransmit a message k times. Protocols using such an acknowledgment scheme are denoted as Positive-Acknowledgment-or-Retransmission (PAR) protocols. A major difficulty in the design of a PAR protocol is the calculation of the timeout, when delays of underlying networks are variable and dynamic [Iren et al., 1999]. In many protocols, the determination of timeouts is based on round-trip time estimations [Karn and Partridge, 1988].

A negative acknowledgment mechanism explicitly identifies messages that have not been received. Since only the sender has knowledge about the points in time when a message has to be transmitted, a negative acknowledgment is only possible when a receivers detects missing sequence numbers when subsequent messages are received. When a sender is not required to send messages in regular intervals, a negative acknowledgment scheme leads to unbounded error recovery times.

In broadcast communication relationships, the construction of distributed processing algorithms can be significantly simplified, if the event-triggered transport protocol provides a globally consistent delivery ordering. The corresponding atomic broadcast protocols operate between the application programs and the broadcast network and isolate the application programs from the unreliable characteristics of the communication network. However, most atomic broadcast protocols involve multiple rounds of message exchanges and introduce significant temporal uncertainty [Kopetz and Kim, 1990]. For example, the reliable broadcast protocols described in [Chang and Maxemchuk, 1984] add latency while forwarding the message to a node that has the permission to establish broadcast orderings. In [Cristian et al., 1985] the delivery latencies depend on the transmission latencies between nodes and the precision of clock synchronization.

Flow Control

Flow control is concerned with balancing the message production rate of the sender with the message consumption rate of the receiver, such that the receiver can follow the sender. A receiver will be unable to process incoming messages in case of unconstrained message arrival rates. The aggregation of event messages in intermediate data structures (e.g., incoming messages queues) will eventually cause omission failures. The purpose of flow control is the prevention of such an overload condition.

Explicit flow control is the predominant type of flow control in event-triggered communication systems. The receiver exerts back pressure on the sender by sending explicit acknowledgment messages. An acknowledgment message informs the sender about the receiver's ability to receive further information.

In a communication system employing explicit flow control, a unidirectional data flow involves a bidirectional control flow. Such an interface is called a *composite interface* [Kopetz, 1999a]. The transmission of a message through the sender depends on a control flow in the opposite direction, i.e. from the receiver to the sender. While a composite interface prevents senders from overloading receivers, correctness of a sender depends on correctness of receivers, which can constitute a problem with respect to error propagation. Furthermore, explicit flow control cannot be applied for events occurring in the natural environment, because it is usually impossible to exert back pressure on the natural environment. Explicit flow control is based on the assumption that sender is within sphere of control of the receiver.

Time-Triggered Communication Systems

A time-triggered communication system is designed for the periodic transmission of state information. It initiates all communication activities at predetermined global points in time. Hence, the temporal behavior of the communication system is controlled solely by the progression of time.

Supported Information Semantics

A time-triggered communication system is designed for the periodic exchange of messages carrying state information. These messages are called *state messages*. The self-contained nature and idempotence of state messages eases the establishment of state synchronization, which does not depend on exactly-once processing guarantees. Since applications are often only interested in the most recent value of a real-time object, old state values can be overwritten with newer state values. Hence, a time-triggered communication system does not require message queues.

Communication Network Interface

As depicted in Figure 2.5 the CNI of a time-triggered communication system acts as a temporal firewall [Kopetz and Nossal, 1997]. The sender can deposit information into the CNI according to the information push paradigm, while the receiver must pull information out of the CNI. A time-triggered transport protocol autonomously carries the state information from the CNI of the sender to the CNIs of the receivers. Since no control signals cross the CNI, temporal fault propagation is prevented by design.

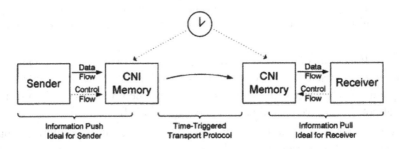

Figure 2.5.   Data Flow (Full Line) and Control Flow (Dashed Line) of a Temporal Firewall Interface [Kopetz, 2001]

The state messages in the CNI memory form two groups. Those state messages that are written by the host application represent the node's service providing linking interface (SPLIF). The communciation controller reads these messages and disseminates them during the slots reserved for the node via the underlying TDMA scheme. Those messages that form the node's service requesting linking interface (SRLIF) are written by the communication controller and read by the host application.

Consistency of information exchanged via the CNI can be ensured by exploiting the a priori knowledge about the points in time when the communication system reads and writes data into the CNI. The host application performs implicit synchronization by establishing a phase alignment between its own CNI accesses and the CNI accesses of the communication controller. A different approach is the use of a synchronization protocol, such as the *Non-Blocking Write Protocol* [Kopetz and Reisinger, 1993].

Transport Protocol

The media access control strategy of a time-triggered communication system is Time Division Multiple Access (TDMA). TDMA statically divides the channel capacity into a number of slots and assigns a unique slot to every node. The communication activities of every node are controlled by a time-triggered communication schedule. The schedule specifies the temporal pattern of messages transmissions, i.e. at what points in time nodes send and receive messages. A sequence of sending slots, which allows every node in an ensemble of n nodes to send exactly once, is called a TDMA round. The sequence of the different TDMA rounds forms the cluster cycle and determines the periodicity of the time-triggered communication.

The a priori knowledge about the times of message exchanges enables the communication system to operate autonomously. The temporal control of communication activities is within the sphere of control of the communication system. Hence, the correct temporal behavior of the communication system is independent of the temporal behavior of the application software in the host computer and can be established in isolation.

Flow Control

Time-triggered communication systems employ *implicit flow control* [Kopetz, 1997]. Sender and receiver agree a priori on the global points in times when messages are exchanged. Based on this knowledge, a component's ability for handling received messages can be ensured at design time, i.e. without acknowledgment messages. Implicit flow control is well-suited for multicast communication relationships, because a unidirectional data flow involves only a unidirectional control flow (*elementary interface* [Kopetz, 1999a]).

Comparative Evaluation

The strengths of event-triggered communication systems are flexibility and a high resource utilization, which enables cost-effective solutions for best-effort systems (e.g., body electronics in a car). Time-triggered communication systems, on the other hand, can provide temporal predictability, composability, and replica determinism. In addition, the a priori knowledge about the points in time of communication activities facilitates the construction of error detection and error containment mechanisms. Consequently, the time-triggered communication paradigm is being accepted for the communication infrastructure of safety-critical applications [Rushby, 2001b]. Examples of time-triggered communication protocols for safety-critical applications are SAFEbus [Hoyme and Driscoll, 1993] (avionic domain), FlexRay [R. Mores et al., 2001] (automotive domain), and TTP [Kopetz and Grünsteidl, 1994] (avionic and automotive domains).

Temporal Predictability

In an event-triggered communication system, the transmission requests of host applications determine the temporal patterns of message exchanges. If multiple host applications request message transmissions in rapid succession (e.g., during peak load scenarios), contention on the network will require the communication system to delay messages. This relationship between communication system load and message transmission latencies can result in significant communication jitter. Another source of communication jitter are retransmission mechanisms employed for handling transient communication failures. Retransmission mechanisms also tend to result in a trashing behavior, i.e. abruptly decreasing throughput with increasing load. If the communication system delays messages, because it can barely handle the message load, a retransmission mechanism will generate additional load when local timeouts elapse.

A time-triggered communication system is based on a static temporal control structure. Since transmission latencies are independent of the event occurrences in the environment and the controlling computer system, the latency jitter is minimized.

Composability

Since an event-triggered communication system is based on external control, the temporal behavior of an event-triggered communication system depends on the points in time of the transmission requests from host applications. Hence, there is an inseparable interrelationship between the compliance to the temporal specification of linking interfaces between components and the component implementations. Compared to time-triggered systems, event-triggered systems provide a weaker separation of architecture and component design.

Time-triggered communication systems support an exact specification of linking interfaces, both in the value domain and time domain, which is a prerequisite for temporal composability [Kopetz and Obermaisser, 2002]. The autonomous control of the communication system isolates the temporal behavior of the communication system from the behavior of the host computers.

Replica Determinism

Fault-free replicated components exhibit replica determinism [Poledna, 1995], if they deliver identical outputs in an identical order within a specified time interval. Replica determinism simplifies the implementation of fault-tolerance by active redundancy, since failures of components can be detected by carrying out a bit-by-bit comparison of the results of replicas. Replica nondeterminism is introduced either by the interface to the real world or the system's internal behavior.

In an event-triggered communication system, a major source for replica nondeterminism are the timeouts of retransmission and acknowledgment mechanisms. If local timeouts are used without global coordination, some replicas can decide locally to timeout, while others will not due to slightly different processing speeds. A further source of replica nondeterminism are inconsistent inputs. If the communication systems does not guarantee a consistent and ordered delivery of input messages, replicas are likely to produce inconsistent output values.

Flexibility

The major strengths of event-triggered communication systems lie in the higher degree of flexibility and the support for a dynamic allocation of resources, which is attractive for variable resource demands. Compared to time-triggered communication systems, an event-triggered communication systems provides fewer a priori restrictions concerning the temporal behavior of nodes. The low static dependencies among components are important, if it is undesirable to make restrictions at design time regarding the addition, removal and replacement of components. An event-triggered communication system eases the migration of functionality between nodes and the addition of functionality that was not anticipated during the system design (extensibility). However, these activities can require the retesting of the temporal behavior of the system, since an event-triggered communication system with external control does not encapsulate the effects of changes in a node.

In a time-triggered communication system, communication slots must either be reserved beforehand in order to allow future extension, or a new communication schedule must be constructed when nodes are added.

Error Detection

In an architecture without replication, error detection is only possible by comparing the actual behavior of a node to some a priori knowledge about the expected behavior. In an event-triggered communication system, the limited a priori knowledge about the communication activities complicates error detection. For example, if a node is not required to send a message at regular intervals, it is not possible to detect a node failure within a bounded latency [Kopetz, 1997].

In a time-triggered communication system the periodic message send times are membership points of the sender [Kopetz et al., 1991]. Every receiver knows a priori when a message of a sender is supposed to arrive, and interprets the arrival of the message as a life sign at the membership point of the sender. From the arrival of the expected messages at two consecutive membership points, it can be concluded that the sender was operational during the interval delimited by these membership points.

Resource Utilization

In an event-triggered communication system, network bandwidth is required only for those messages, for which dissemination is requested by the host applications. Bandwidth that is not consumed by a node is available to other nodes, thus enabling the statistical multiplexing of bandwidth. This approach allows the dimensioning of resources according to average demands, which is desirable for non critical communication activities, where a resource-adequacy policy would not be cost-effective.

In a time-triggered communication system all communication activities are fixed and planned for the specified peak load demand. Hence, the resource utilization of an event-triggered communication system will be better than that of a comparable time-triggered communication system, if load conditions are low or average. However, for safety-critical applications a resource adequacy policy is required anyway in order to guarantee safety during peak load scenarios.

Specification of Interfaces during the Design Process

The design of distributed embedded systems is often viewed as a top-down approach, which proceeds via well-defined levels of abstraction [Pires et al., 1993]. The specification serves as the input description for the designer. The specification provides the definition of the common behavior of the system by describing the interactions between the system and its environment in the temporal and value domain. The specification is transformed into a functional description, which is given as a set of explicit or implicit relations which involve inputs, outputs and possibly internal information [Edwards et al., 1997]. The functional specification is mapped to an architecture by performing a decomposition of functions and assigning resulting functional units to components.

This section compares differences in the design process of distributed real-time systems, depending on whether a functional specification is mapped to an event-triggered or a time-triggered system architecture. The major difference between event-triggered and time-triggered architectures lies in the level of rigidity in the temporal specification of linking interfaces during the mapping of a functional specification to an architecture. A time-triggered system specifies the precise points in time of information exchanges with respect to a global time base. Event-triggered systems can establish flexibility and high average performance by employing a weaker temporal specification of interfaces. Examples for such temporal specifications are deterministic or probabilistic message interarrival and service times.

Time-Triggered Systems

The main design principle of a time-triggered system is the separation of local and global concerns. Global concerns are the subject of architecture design, during which the decomposition of the system into components and the specification of the component interfaces is performed. Component design focuses on local concerns of the application in a node, such as task scheduling.

If a system can be developed without legacy components, then a top-down decomposition will be pursued. During the architecture design phase the application is decomposed into a set of clusters and nodes. A systematic fault-tolerance concept is devised for internal physical faults of nodes. Sets of nodes that compute the same function are logically grouped into fault-tolerant units. A fault-tolerant unit will tolerate the failure of any of its independent constituent nodes without a degradation of service. The number of nodes required for the construction of a fault-tolerant unit depends on the assumed failure modes. For example, the consistent failure of a single node can be masked by a fault-tolerant unit consisting of three nodes (triple modular redundancy). The nodes operate in replica determinism [Poledna, 1995] and present their results to a voter (located at every consumer of the result) that makes a majority decision.

After the decomposition has been completed, the CNIs of nodes are specified in the value and time domain. The state variables that are to be exchanged via the time-triggered communication system are identified and the admissible temporal accuracy intervals [Kopetz and Kim, 1990] are determined. The size of a temporal accuracy interval is determined by the dynamics of the real-time entities in the controlled object. Given these data, a cluster compiler [Kopetz and Nossal, 1995] can construct a time-triggered schedule for the communication system. At the end of the architecture design phase, the precise interface specifications of components are available, which are the inputs and constraints for the component design.

During the component design phase, the development of the host application software is performed. The precise specification of the CNI to the time-triggered communication system provides pre- and post-conditions for the application software. The host operating system can employ any reasonable scheduling strategy, as long as it ensures the timely update of the state information in the CNI in order to ensure temporal accuracy of the state information transferred to other nodes. Furthermore, in case of phase-sensitive real-time images [Kopetz, 1997], the host operating system must schedule tasks in such a way that temporal accuracy of the received state variables is guaranteed.

Event-Triggered Systems

During the design of event-triggered systems, a functional specification is mapped to an event-triggered architecture, which employs an event-triggered communication system for the establishment of the linking interface between components. Since message exchanges occur as a consequence to events, event-triggered systems offer an interrelationship between communication and computations. Hence, there is also an interrelationship between architecture and component design.

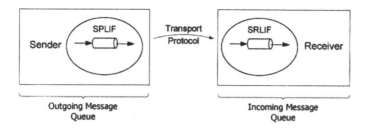

Figure 2.6. Event-Triggered Linking Interface

Compared to time-triggered systems, event-triggered systems do not require a specification of the precise global points in time of message exchanges. This weaker temporal specification enables the communication system to allow for contention and to multiplex communication resources among components. A temporal specification of the linking interfaces of components is, however, necessary to dimension buffers of an event-triggered communication system.

Figure 2.6 shows two components connected via an event-triggered linking interface. Message queues serve the purpose of buffering outgoing messages that are delayed through contention at the network, as well as incoming messages that have not yet been fetched by the application. It is not possible to dimension message queues in case of unconstrained message arrival rates, thereby leading to potential message omissions and loss of state synchronization for messages with event semantics. In order to be able to dimension outgoing queues, the temporal specification of the sender's linking interface must provide a statement about the message production rate of the sender. The production rate of the sender corresponds to the interarrival times of messages at the communication system. Equally, in order to dimension the incoming queue at the receiver, one requires a statement about the consumption rate of the receiver in relation to the sender's production rate. The consumption rate of the receiver corresponds to the service times of messages received from the communication system.

2.5   Computational Models

If large numbers of computers are to work together in computing systems, then it is necessary to have a system-wide architecture and computational model that they all support [Treleaven and Hopkins, 1981]. This section describes prevalent com-

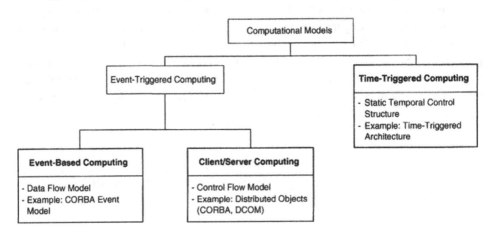

Figure 2.7. Hierarchy of Prevalent Computational Models

putational models for the representation and analysis of the design of distributed computer systems: event-based, client/server, and time-triggered computing (see Figure 2.7). We will describe the requirements for an underlying platform (communication infrastructure, hosts) and the application areas of these computational models with an emphasis on the applicability for the construction of real-time systems.

Event-Based Computing

In *event-based models*, the glue that ties together distributed components is an event notification service (or event service). An *event notification service* is an application-independent infrastructure, whereby generators of events publish event notifications to the infrastructure and consumers of events subscribe with the infrastructure to receive relevant notifications [Carzaniga et al., 1999]. An event notification service distinguishes between the role of an event supplier and the role of event consumer. An event supplier asynchronously communicates event data to a group of event consumers as depicted in Figure 2.8. The component interactions are

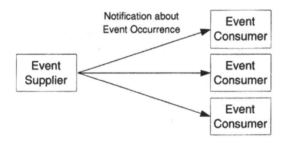

Figure 2.8.   Event-Based Communication

modeled as asynchronous occurrences and responses to events. In order to inform other components about the occurrence of an internal event (a state change), components send notifications containing information about that event. Upon receiving a notification, a component can react by performing actions that, in turn, may result in the occurrence of other events [Carzaniga et al., 1999].

At the communication infrastructure, event notifications result in the sporadic transmission of event messages. Event messages carry event information and are triggered by the occurrence of the corresponding event. Hence, event-based models require an event-triggered communication service as the communication infrastructure for the transport of event notifications.

Data and Control Flow

Event-based models correspond to the *data flow model* [Veen, 1986]. The event notifications in event-based models represent a combination of control and data flow. Event information received by an event consumer represents input data that triggers computations, often in combination with other event notifications.

In the data flow model, a computation is represented by directed graphs, which illustrates the flow of data between operations. The nodes in this directed graph represent the operations, edges represent data paths. Data flow is a distributed model of computation, i.e. there is no single location of control. Furthermore, data flow is an asynchronous model that allows the execution of an operation when all input data is available. In the directed graph, the availability of inputs is indicated by a data token on each of the input arcs of a node. Data tokens represent partial results, which are consumed by the execution of an operation. Since executions use up input data tokens, these tokens are no longer available as input to other executions. The computational results of an operation are represented by releasing result tokens. The data flow model provides no concept of shared data. Precedence constraints between computational activities are expressed via the flow of data. Since an operation is activated only by the availability of input data it depends on, the overall computation is inherently parallel and asynchronous.

When building a system based on the distributed data flow model, a mapping between suppliers and consumers is required at the level of the underlying communication infrastructure. This mapping ensures that the event data of the correct supplier forms the input to a particular computational activity at a consumer. The mapping between suppliers and consumers can occur either statically or dynamically. In case of a static mapping, the different data flows are identified at design-time. A dynamic mapping allows consumers to express interest in a particular event at run-time. A dynamic mapping also enables producers to announce the availability of a particular class of events at run-time. For example, *publish-subscribe models* [Busi and Zavattaro, 2001] provide such a dynamic mapping between suppliers and consumers. In publish-subscribe models a consumer registers at a supplier (or a mediator) in order to request the delivery of future events from the supplier.

Example – CORBA Event Model

An example of a distributed event-based architecture is the Common Object Request Broker Architecture (CORBA) Event Model [OMG, 2002b] by the Object Management Group (OMG) (also called CORBA notification service). This model constructs a publish-subscribe model on top of a client/server architecture. Both suppliers and consumers are CORBA clients and use event channels that are part of the notification service for exchanging event data. Transported event data can be unstructured or structured. In the latter case, the structure is described by the OMG Interface Definition Language (IDL) [OMG, 2002a]. A single event channel can support multiple suppliers and consumers. Furthermore, event channels can consume information of other event channels, which results in the composition of event channels.

In order to limit the load resulting from events, the CORBA notification service applies filtering. Filter objects incorporate a set of constraints, which represent boolean filtering expressions. The filtering expressions are specified in a dedicated constraint language. Filter objects can be used both at the supplier and the consumer side. They can also be composed to perform hierarchical filtering.

An application of an event-based model for real-time systems is the real-time CORBA event service described in [Harrison et al., 1997]. This work extends the CORBA notification service with support for event correlation by combining several events with conjunctive or disjunctive semantics. In addition, the real-time CORBA event service offers object-oriented event dispatching and priority scheduling. The dispatcher uses priorities for handling events from suppliers. When the dispatcher receives a supplier event, it queries the run-time scheduler to determine the priority of the consumer the event is destined for. This priority value determines the priority queue into which the event is inserted. The dispatcher supports the preemption of running threads in order to dispatch a high priority event immediately. In addition, the real-time CORBA event service provides an event channel with a non-preemptive earliest-deadline first scheduling strategy that does not use event priorities.

Client/Server Computing

In the *client/server computing paradigm,* one or more clients and one or more servers, along with the underlying operating system and interprocess communication systems, form a composite system allowing distributed computations [Sinha, 1992]. Clients send requests to a server, which processes the client requests and returns the results. Clients and servers typically run on different computers interconnected by a network [Maffeis, 1998] that is responsible for transferring requests from clients to servers and responses from servers to clients.

In real-time systems, correctness of a client/server interaction depends not only on the value of the result returned by the server, but also on the temporal behavior between the request and the corresponding result. The temporal behavior can be described with three parameters [Kopetz, 1997]: The minimum time between two successive requests by clients, the maximum response time expected by the client that issues a request, and the worst-case execution time of the server for processing the request.

Data and Control Flow

The client/server computing paradigm corresponds to the *control flow model* [Treleaven and Hopkins, 1981]. In contrast to the data flow computational models, control flow models separate the flow of data and control. This separation is beneficial, if specific control patterns are required. A system can be described by a directed graph, with nodes representing computations. An arc between two nodes denotes a control flow between these nodes. In the graph representation, control tokens must be present at the input arcs of a node for an operation to be executable. The execution of an operation releases control tokens on output arcs, thereby enabling the execution of successive operations.

Example – Distributed Objects

Distributed object computing is the application of the client/server model to object-based programming. In distributed object computing, objects are pieces of software that encapsulate an internal state and make it accessible through a well defined interface (remote procedure calling). One of the widely adopted, vendor independent distributed object computing standards is the OMG CORBA specification [OMG, 2002a].

Time-Triggered Computing

The *time-triggered model of computation* [Kopetz, 1998b] aims at the representation and analysis of the design of large hard real-time systems. The time-triggered model of computation is based on time and timeliness of real-time information. It partitions a distributed computer system into nearly autonomous subsystems with small and stable interfaces between these subsystems. A time-triggered communication system connects the interfaces. The time-triggered communication system performs a periodic exchange of state messages. Through the use of state semantics, a new version of a state message can replace the previous one in the interface.

Data and Control Flow

The interface between the host and the communication system is the temporal firewall interface [Kopetz and Nossal, 1997], which represents a data sharing interface with state information semantics. The syntactic structure of the data items in the temporal firewall and the global points in time when the data items in the temporal firewall are accessed by the time-triggered communication system are a priori specified. No control signals pass a temporal firewall, which results in the independence of the temporal behavior of the host and the time-triggered communication system.

The obligations of the host application consist of the update (producer obligation) and use (consumer obligation) of the real-time images in the temporal firewall. It is the obligation of the host application to update the state information in the temporal firewall to maintain temporal accuracy. Based on the a priori knowledge about the temporal accuracy of the real-time images in the temporal firewall, the consumer must sample the information in the temporal firewall with a sampling rate that ensures that the accessed real-time image is temporally accurate at its time of use.

Example

An example for an architecture adhering to the time-triggered model of computation is the Time-Triggered Architecture (TTA) [Kopetz and Bauer, 2003], which provides a computing infrastructure for the design and implementation of dependable distributed real-time systems. The services and design principles of the TTA are presented in Section 5.1. The TTA also provides the foundation for the integrated system architecture that is introduced in this book. This integrated system architecture supports both the event-triggered and time-triggered models of computation.

2.6 Distributed System Architectures for Ultra-Dependable Systems

This section gives an overview of distributed system architectures for ultra-dependable real-time systems: Spring [Stankovic, 1990], Multicomputer Architecture for Fault-Tolerance (MAFT) [Kieckhafer et al., 1988], Integrated Modular Avionics (IMA) [ARINC 651, 1991], and BASEMENT [Hansson et al., 1997]. For each system architecture, we describe the corresponding system structure, i.e. the constituting parts and the system topology. Furthermore, we discuss the communication system that interconnects the components to the overall system and analyze the services provided at the component level, such as task scheduling. Finally, we relate each architecture to the computational models introduced in Section 2.5.

Spring

The Spring architecture [Stankovic, 1990] is designed for large, complex, distributed safety-critical real-time systems. As many real-time systems are mixed-criticality systems, Spring distinguishes computations and communication along their criticality levels. A priori guarantees are provided for safety-critical activities, while best-effort guarantees are available for activities of lower criticality.

System Structure

The Spring architecture is composed of a network of multiprocessor nodes. The constituent parts of a node are a system processor, a communications processor, one or more application processors, and an I/O subsystem.

1 **System Processor:** The system processor executes the scheduling algorithm and supports the operating system services, thus reducing operating system overhead in the application processors. In addition, the system processor handles high-priority interrupts by adapting the execution plans constructed by the scheduler.

2 **Communications Processor:** The communications processor is responsible for the exchange of information between nodes.

3 **Application Processors:** One or more application processors execute the application tasks as specified by the execution plan constructed by the scheduler in the system processor. In case a system processor fails, an application processor is reconfigured to replace the system processor.

4 **I/O Subsystem:** The I/O subsystem handles low-priority interrupts and accesses I/O devices.

Communication System

As described in [Nahum et al., 1992], the communication service of the Spring architecture enables tasks to exchange messages. Tasks may communicate with other tasks running on the same processor, with tasks on different processors in the same node, and with tasks on processors of different nodes. The same communication primitives are used, independently of the location of the communicating tasks.

Tasks communicate with each other by placing messages into ports, which is denoted as *queuing*. Task remove messages from ports by performing receive operations *(dequeuing)*. Each message can have a deadline, which denotes when the message must be delivered to the receive port. Ports are described by the following properties:

- **Capacity:** The capacity of a port determines the maximum number of messages that can be stored in the port.

- **Queuing Policy:** A port's queuing policy determines the order, in which messages are stored and retrieved.

- **Overflow Policy:** The overflow policy determines the actions (e.g., discarding the message) in case a message arrives at a port with insufficient storage capacity.

- **Task Type:** Ports are owned by tasks of a particular criticality level. The task type is employed for the scheduling of communication activities, thus preventing a task of lower criticality from affecting a task with higher criticality.

- **Semantic Type:** Spring supports three semantic types: synchronous, asynchronous, and request/reply. In synchronous communication, the sender task blocks until the receiver dequeues the message from its receive port. In asynchronous communication, senders do not wait for the dequeuing of a message at the receiver. Furthermore, a receiver does not wait for the availability of messages in asynchronous communication. Request/reply semantics support client/server interactions, i.e. a request from the client results in a corresponding reply from the server.

If tasks are located on different nodes, the network connections occur through real-time virtual circuits and real-time datagrams. *Real-time virtual circuits* are dedicated channels with guaranteed maximum latencies. For safety-critical tasks, real-time virtual circuits are pre-allocated. *Real-time datagrams* provide a best-effort communication service. These datagrams attempt to deliver messages within their deadlines without providing guarantees.

In [Teo, 1995] the Spring communication service has been extended to group communication. In synchronous multicast groups, the scheduler ensures that communicating tasks are scheduled in such a way, that messages are always ready when a receive operation is performed. Group membership must be static for synchronous multicast groups, i.e. no tasks may join a group at run-time. Asynchronous multicast groups offer higher flexibility and scheduling is performed at run-time. Asynchronous multicast groups provide, however, only best-effort guarantees for meeting message deadlines.

Component Level

Each node in the Spring architecture runs the Spring Kernel [Stankovic and Ramamritham, 1989]. The Spring Kernel provides system primitives with bounded worst-case execution times for task management, scheduling, memory management, and intertask communication.

The Spring Kernel supports three types of tasks:

1 **Critical tasks** must meet their deadlines, otherwise a catastrophic result might occur. Resources are a priori reserved for critical tasks. The Spring architecture is based on the assumption that the overall number of critical tasks is small in relation to the overall number of tasks.

2 **Essential tasks** possess timing constraints and degrade the performance of the system, if these timing constrains are not met. For economic reasons and to improve flexibility, essential tasks do not use a pre-allocation of resources. The Spring scheduling algorithm dynamically searches for a feasible schedule that maximizes the value of executed tasks. The value of a task is its full importance value, if it completes before its deadline and a diminished value (e.g., negative value or zero), if it does not make its deadline.

3 **Non-essential tasks** execute when they do not impact critical or essential tasks.

In order to avoid unpredictable blocking, each task acquires resources before it begins and releases the resources upon completion. Tasks are characterized by precedence relationships, resource requirements, importance levels, worst-case execution times, and deadlines. Tasks with a common deadline can be grouped into a task group, thereby reducing the scheduling overhead.

The Spring scheduler is composed of four levels. At the lowest level, a dispatcher for each application processor removes tasks from scheduling queues, called system task tables. For each application processor, the system task table encodes previously established scheduling decisions that incorporate a proper task order for guaranteeing all precedence and timing constraints. The second scheduling level is a local scheduler, which uses the parameters of the current task set for deciding whether a new task or task group can be scheduled locally. The third level is a distributed scheduler that tries to find a node to execute a task or task group. The fourth level is a meta-level controller that adapts to significant changes in the environment by switching scheduling algorithms.

Supported Computational Models

The Spring architecture aims at event-triggered computing, i.e. control signals are not restricted to the progression of time. Computational and communication activities are initiated through interrupts, which represent service requests from the environment. To preserve predictability in case of indeterministic environments, Spring employs functional partitioning by separating computational resources for application software and interrupt handling. Interrupts are handled by the I/O subsystem and the system processor, thus affecting the application only indirectly via the scheduler.

MAFT

Multicomputer Architecture for Fault-Tolerance (MAFT) [Kieckhafer et al., 1988] is a distributed computer architecture for ultra-dependable systems. MAFT focuses on high reliability and high performance. The minimum performance objectives of MAFT have been derived from the requirements of flight-control systems.

System Structure

A MAFT system consists of node computers interconnected by a broadcast bus network. Each node is partitioned into two separate processors called the operations controller and the application processor. The operations controller is responsible for communication, synchronization, data voting, error detection, task scheduling, and system reconfiguration. The application processor executes the application programs.

MAFT allows to redistribute application workload to support graceful degradation of application functions as resources are lost. A task reconfiguration algorithm [Kieckhafer et al., 1988] establishes an eligibility table, which denotes for each task to which nodes the task can be assigned. The reconfiguration algorithm is implemented with three independent processes. The *Global Task Activation Process* activates or deactivates tasks, thus accounting for changes in the number of available nodes. The *Task Reallocation Process* reallocates tasks among the operating nodes. The *Task-Node Status Matching Process* prevents tasks from being executed on particular nodes.

Communication System

The communication between the operations controller and the application processor occurs through an asynchronous parallel interface. The communication between operations controllers occurs via the broadcast bus network. Four types of messages are exchanged on this network:

- **Data Messages:** A data message is broadcast by the operations controller, whenever it receives a computed data value from its own application processor.

- **Scheduling Messages:** In MAFT, precedence constraints between tasks are expressed via concurrent forks/joins and conditional branches. In order to control the distributed task scheduling, MAFT establishes a consistent view on scheduling data, i.e. the tasks that have finished execution. Byzantine agreement on scheduling data occurs through the exchange of scheduling messages that denote that an application processor has completed an application task. An interactive consistency algorithm operates in synchronized transmission rounds, during which nodes rebroadcast the scheduling data received in the previous round. The required number of rounds depends on the assumed number of simultaneous malicious faults.

- **Synchronization Messages:** The clock synchronization of MAFT employs an interactive convergence algorithm [Srikanth and Toueg, 1987]. Clock synchronization is based on the exchange of synchronization messages whose transmission implicitly denotes the local clock times. A fault-tolerant voting algorithm produces voted timestamp values for adjusting local clocks.

- **Error-Management Messages:** Error handling in MAFT is based on a penalty counting mechanism. Each node maintains a base penalty count for every other node. Furthermore, the operations controller continuously monitors the behavior of all nodes and calculates an incremental penalty count. The incremental penalty count denotes the proposed penalty assessment, based on the error detections of the current *atomic period*. At the beginning of every atomic period, each node broadcasts an error report message containing error flags, the base penalty counter, the incremental penalty counter, and an identification of suspected nodes. Each node votes on the contents of the error report messages and updates its base penalty count. If a certain threshold of the base penalty count is exceeded, the operations controllers recommend the exclusion of a node from the operating set.

Each operations controller stores a copy of all shared application data values. In addition, the operations controller performs voting of data values, transparently to application processors. Voting is performed "on-the-fly" by using a newly received data value and any previously received copies. Reasonableness checks filter out data which is outside of predefined maximum and minimum limits. MAFT supports different approximate voting algorithms, such as the "median select" algorithm and the "mean of the medial extremes" algorithm. Byzantine agreement and converging algorithms allow to maintain agreement even in case a node behaves maliciously faulty.

Component Level

For scheduling, MAFT employs a fault-tolerant variation of the deterministic priority-list algorithm. Each task possesses a unique priority number. When an application processor becomes available, the highest priority ready task on the application processor is selected for execution.

The MAFT scheduler treats all tasks as periodic. The period of each task is a multiple of the atomic period. The boundaries between atomic periods coincide with the transmissions of synchronization messages. Non-periodic behavior is obtained through conditional branching.

Supported Computational Model

MAFT supports both the event-triggered and time-triggered paradigms for communication activities. When the application controller passes data values to its operations controller, it thereby triggers the transmission of a data message. Consequently, the transmission of data occurs event-triggered, since transmissions are within the sphere of control of the application software in the application controller.

For error handling and clock synchronization, on the other hand, periodic time-triggered disseminations of error-management messages (penalty counts, error flags) and system state messages are employed. These messages are exchanged in every atomic period.

Integrated Modular Avionics

ARINC standard 651 [ARINC 651, 1991] is known as Integrated Modular Avionics (IMA) and addresses the design of architectures aimed at the separate implementation and integration of avionic applications. As depicted in Figure 2.9, the construction of an IMA architecture relies on several other ARINC standards. The services of the avionic software environment are specified by ARINC 653 [ARINC 653, 2003], which is known as APplication EXecutive (APEX). APEX provides services for partition management, process management, time management, memory management, interpartition communication, intrapartition communication, and diagnosis.

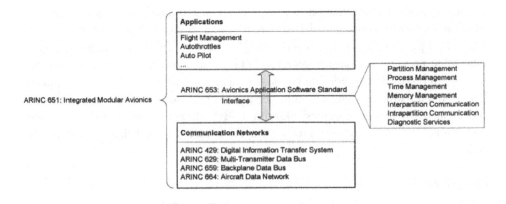

Figure 2.9. Integrated Modular Avionics

IMA systems are not restricted to a particular communication network. Common standards for the communication network include point-to-point protocols such as ARINC 429 [ARINC 429, 2001], event-triggered communication systems (e.g., ARINC 664 [ARINC 664 – Part 7, 2003], ARINC 629 [ARINC 629, 1991]), and time-triggered communication systems (e.g., ARINC 659 (SAFEbus) [ARINC 659, 1993]).

Consequently, IMA architectures are not restricted to a particular computational model. In combination with a time-triggered communication service, such as ARINC 659, an IMA architecture supports time-triggered computing with computational and communicational activities being controlled by the progression of time. In conjunction with an event-triggered communication service, such as ARINC 664, the resulting system adheres to an event-triggered computational model.

In this section, we will focus on an IMA architecture that employs the ARINC 664 implementation Avionics Full Duplex Switched Ethernet (AFDX) [ARINC 664 – Part 7, 2003]. Such an architecture allows an event-based design, in which computational and communication activities are triggered by the occurrence of significant events. The switched star network AFDX is an example of an event-triggered network complying with the ARINC 664 standard for aircraft data networks.

System Structure

With ARINC 664, the aeronautical industry explains requirements and solutions for applying standard communications protocols complying to the Open System Interconnection (OSI) Reference Model [International Standardization Organisation, 1994] for avionics applications. Consequently, ARINC 664 adopts the structuring of protocols into layers and the OSI concept of peer-to-peer communication. Each layer understands the interfaces to adjacent layers, but has no knowledge of what is occurring in other layers (see Figure 2.10).

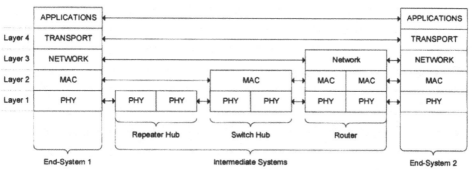

Figure 2.10. Peer-to-Peer Communications through Intermediate Systems [ARINC 664 – Part 1, 2002]

An ARINC 664 network consists of two entities: *end-systems* and *intermediate systems*. An end-system is a component that serves as a source or receptor of data

on a network, while intermediate systems implement the network. End-systems
are interconnected through repeater hubs, switch hubs, and routers. A *repeater hub*
forwards messages between segments. It does not perform filtering, i.e. forwarding
to a segment is performed independently whether a message is destined for an end-
system on the segment or not. Consequently, a repeater hub connects multiple
segments into a common logical bus forming a single collision domain. A *switch
hub* interconnects multiple segments into a single network at OSI layer 2. By
looking at the Media Access Control (MAC) addresses (layer 2 addresses), a switch
hub only relays traffic to a segment, if messages are destined for this network. A
router operates on the Internet Protocol (IP) layer and changes the MAC destination
address to the appropriate next hop, which is either an end-system or another router.

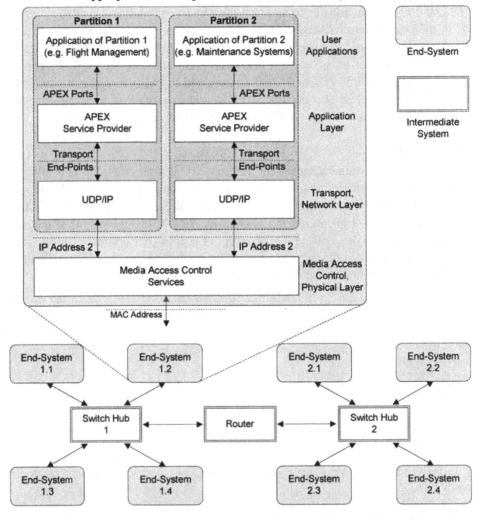

Figure 2.11. Example of an ARINC 664 Aircraft Data Network

Figure 2.11 gives an overview of an IMA system that is based on ARINC 664. The system consists of two ARINC 664 compliant subnetworks interconnected by a router. A subnetwork is composed of end-systems, each containing one or more partitions. Partitions execute application software and provide protection against the effects of software faults in other partitions. The operating environment for application software conforms to ARINC specification 653 [ARINC 653, 2003]. APEX defines the interface between the operating system and applications. Application software accesses logical communication channels via so-called APEX ports. The APEX services are part of the core software in each end-system and map the channels of APEX into end-points of the User Datagram Protocol (UDP) transport service provided by ARINC 664.

Communication System

APEX defines *channels* for interpartition communication through the exchange of messages. The destination for messages exchanged through a channel is a partition, not a process (see Figure 2.12). Communication activities are independent

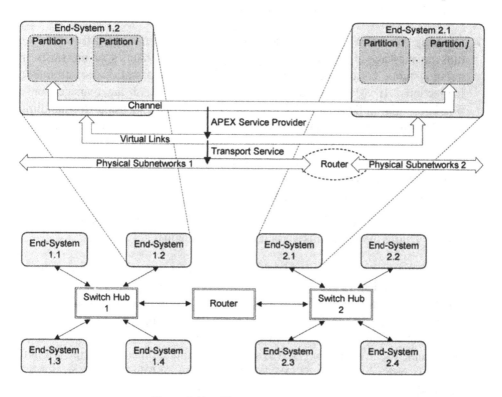

Figure 2.12. Channels and Virtual Links

of the location of both source and destination partitions. A partition can communicate via multiple channels. A channel is configured by the system integrator and possesses one sending port and one or more receiving ports. Each port is assigned a port name, which should refer to the data exchanged via the port rather than to the producer/consumer. Furthermore, a port is assigned a transfer direction (send or receive). A port can support either event or state semantics through operating in one of the following two transfer modes:

- **Sampling Mode:** Successive messages contain identical but updated data. Received messages overwrite old information, thus requiring no message queuing. Sampling mode assumes that applications are only interested in the most recent version of a message. A validity indicator denotes whether the age of the copied message is consistent with the required refresh rate defined for the port. The information semantics of messages in sampling mode corresponds to the concept of state information as introduced in Section 2.1.

  In sampling mode, a channel is assigned a single send port and one or more receive ports. Messages must possess a fixed length and arrive with a minimum frequency, as specified via the port's required refresh rate.

- **Queuing Mode:** Messages are assumed to contain uniquely different data, thus no message should be lost. The information semantics of messages in queuing mode corresponds to the concept of event information as introduced in Section 2.1. Messages are buffered in queues, which are managed on a first-in/first-out (FIFO) basis. Application software is responsible for handling overflowing queues. If a queue is full, a sending task can either cancel the send request or enter waiting state. In the latter case, the task is delayed until the queue can store the message and the task is scheduled again during the partition's time slice. Equally, a receiving task can either block when issuing a receive request on an empty queue or cancel the receive request.

  In queuing mode, a channel is assigned a single send port and a single receive port. Queuing mode permits variable message lengths.

The concept of channels, as used for interpartition communication according to APEX, is independent of the actual transport mechanism. While a time-triggered communication system simplifies the establishment of temporal validity in sampling mode, event-triggered communication systems natively support sporadic transmissions of event messages as required in queuing mode.

An example for an event-triggered avionic communication system is the ARINC 664 example implementation AFDX. AFDX is based on Ethernet and provides a dual redundant, switched star network. AFDX does not assume that transmitting end-systems are synchronized, but assumes a bounded interarrival time distribution of message transmission requests from end-systems. This assumption can be applied for limiting the effects of a faulty end-system on messages from other end-systems. AFDX interconnects end-systems through *virtual links*. A virtual link is a communication object with one source end-system within the avionics network and one or more destination end-systems. Regardless of activities of other end-systems, a virtual link provides a guaranteed bandwidth, bounded maximum latencies and jitter, a defined probability of frame loss, and impersonation protection.

- **Guaranteed Bandwidth and Maximum Latency:** A virtual link is assigned a *bandwidth allocation gap* d_{BAG}, which is the minimum space between the first bits of two consecutive frames. The length of the bandwidth allocation gap d_{BAG} ranges between 1 ms and 128 ms with $d_{BAG} = 2^k$ ms ($0 \leqslant k < 8$). The maximum bandwidth usable by a virtual link results from its bandwidth allocation gap and the maximum frame size L^{max}. The maximum usable bandwidth is L^{max}/d_{BAG}.

- **Maximum Jitter:** A virtual link exhibits jitter that is introduced by the switch. Jitter depends on the load and the configuration, in particular the number of virtual links. The maximum jitter is guaranteed to be less than $500 \mu s$.

- **Defined Probability of Frame Loss:** AFDX supports redundant communication channels through a "first valid wins" policy. Transmitted Ethernet frames are assigned sequence numbers, which enable a receiver to remove frames that represent redundant copies. The first frame with a valid sequence number is accepted.

- **Impersonation Protection:** AFDX prevents an end-system from sending Ethernet frames with the source address of another end-system.

Component Level

At the component level, ARINC specification 653 distinguishes between *core software* and *application software*. The core software is responsible for mapping the APEX Application Programming Interface (API) onto the underlying platform, e.g., implementing channels through the available transport mechanisms. If the core software employs fragmentation, sequencing, routing, or message redundancy, these mechanism have to be transparent to the application software.

Each end-system contains one or more *partitions*. A partition is a set of functionally separated tasks with their associated context and configuration data. The tasks of a partition and the required resources are statically defined. The scheduling of these tasks occurs via two-level scheduling. On the first level, partitions are scheduled by the progression of time. Partitions do not have priorities and are activated relative to a time frame. As the time frame can be synchronized to the underlying communication system, the activation of partitions can also be synchronized to the communication system. Tasks within partitions possess priorities, which are used for dynamic task scheduling. If a partition is active, the scheduler selects the ready task with the highest priority for execution – preempting task's with lower priorities.

APEX distinguishes four types of software modules. The application partitions and the system partitions form the application software. The core software consists of the O/S kernel and system-specific functions.

- **Application partitions** execute software implementing application functionality. For error containment reasons, application partitions may only use ARINC 653 calls to interface the hardware and communication system.

- **System partitions** require interfaces outside of APEX services. System partitions are specific to the core software implementation.

- **The O/S kernel** provides the services defined by the APEX specification.

- **System-specific functions** implement device drivers, diagnostic, and maintenance functions.

Tasks within partitions can employ intrapartition communication mechanisms, thereby avoiding the runtime overhead of message passing. Intrapartition communication mechanisms include buffers, blackboards, semaphores, and events. Buffers and blackboards allow general communication and synchronization between tasks in a partition, while semaphores and events are used for synchronization only.

In order to protect the memory of partitions and to avoid interference in the temporal domain (e.g., through a task overrunning its deadline or blocking a shared resource), APEX demands sufficient processing, I/O and memory resources from the used processor. Furthermore, APEX requires time resources, atomic operations, and mechanisms for transferring control to the operating system, if a partition attempts to perform an invalid operation.

Supported Computational Models

IMA is not limited to a particular computational model, although the services of the underlying platform (operating system and communication system) determine the ability for supporting a computational model. For example, the availability of clock synchronization is a prerequisite for time-triggered computing.

The APEX API allows application software to explicitly request message transmissions. No distinction is made by APEX between periodic and aperiodic messages. In conjunction with an event-triggered communication system with external control, such as the ARINC 664 sample implementation AFDX, these transmission requests lead to on-demand communication activities at the network.

For handling messages with event information, APEX offers a queuing mode in order to ensure the exactly-once processing of messages. Queuing mode facilitates the establishment of state synchronization in case of messages with event information, as messages are buffered in intermediate buffers. To avoid buffer overflows, ARINC 664 proposes an error indication that is sent to transmitting applications.

APEX supports event-triggered task activations, as tasks can wait for significant events, such as the arrival of a message from the communication system. In queuing-mode, receiver tasks can block until a message arrives in a queue, thus allowing computations to be triggered by the occurrence of events.

Sampling mode aims at the exchange of messages containing state information. A validity indicator is associated with each port operating in sampling mode. The validity indicator denotes whether the age of the copied message is consistent with the required refresh rate of a port, i.e. the temporal accuracy of the real-time image provided through the port. Sampling mode forms the basis for the development of applications conforming to the time-triggered model of computation. However, the event-triggered ARINC 664 example implementation AFDX exhibits communication jitter up to **500 μs.** In distributed control systems without a global time base, communication jitter leads to an uncertainty about the instant a real-time entity was observed and can be expressed as an additional error in the value domain, if there is knowledge about the maximum rate of change of the real-time entity. The communication jitter ε also limits the achievable precision of a global time base for AFDX. It is not possible to internally synchronize the clocks of an ensemble of N nodes to a better precision than $\Pi = \varepsilon \cdot \left(1 - \frac{1}{N}\right)$ [Lundelius-Welch and Lynch, 1984].

BASEMENT

In the Vehicle Internal Architecture (VIA) research project, the BASE-MENT [Hansson et al., 1997] system architecture has been designed for safety-critical automotive systems. DACAPO is a realization of BASEMENT for ultra-dependable applications [Rostamzadeh et al., 1995], which has been developed in collaboration with car manufacturers. BASEMENT distinguishes between two types of applications, namely safety-critical applications and non safety-critical applications. If an application has stringent timing constraints specified via deadlines and a failure to meet such a deadline can potentially lead to an accident, the corresponding application is denoted as safety-critical. Otherwise, the application is non safety-critical.

System Structure

A BASEMENT system consists of a set of node computers interconnected with a communication network. A node computer possesses a network interface and sensors/actuators for interfacing the controlled object. In order to increase reliability, BASEMENT proposes internal redundancy of node computers and redundant networks.

Communication System

The communication system of BASEMENT divides time into slots. A subset of the available slots is statically assigned to nodes for performing the message exchanges of safety-critical applications. The allocation of slots to nodes is performed by an off-line scheduling tool [Hansson and Sjödin, 1995]. BASEMENT supports different communication modes with corresponding precomputed communication schedules. The switching of communication modes occurs dynamically.

The remaining slots are available for non safety-critical applications and can be dynamically allocated to nodes. In the CAN-based prototype implementation of BASEMENT, contention in these communication slots is resolved by the CAN hardware arbitration mechanism.

Component Level

Tasks for safety-critical applications are periodic. The scheduling of safety-critical application tasks is controlled by a static, cyclic schedule, which is created by an off-line scheduling tool [Hansson and Sjödin, 1995]. For each node, this tools constructs a dedicated schedule that encodes all precedence requirements and statically defines the resource allocations. Computational activities are synchronized to a global time base. The length of the generated schedule is the systolic base time. At run-time, the operating system kernel ensures that the generated schedule is followed.

Tasks for non safety-critical applications are periodic or aperiodic. These tasks are scheduled by a preemptive priority driven scheduler. BASEMENT supports both dynamic and static priority assignment. No guarantees are given that deadlines of non safety-critical tasks are met.

Supported Computational Models

BASEMENT supports both the event-triggered and time-triggered computational models. Safety-critical applications employ time-triggered communication and computational activities based on a statically constructed schedule.

Non safety-critical applications can employ event-triggered communication activities with contention between nodes. Non safety-critical application tasks are usually initiated event-driven, thus reacting to the occurrence of external events.

Furthermore, the BASEMENT architecture introduces a data flow model that is based on a hardware metaphor of software. In analogy with hardware circuits, software modules are termed *software circuits* [Hansson et al., 1997]. Software circuit communication via connectors and are combined to form larger software circuits. Each software circuit possesses one or more input and output connectors. The execution of a software circuit is enabled when appropriate data is available at all input connectors. When the software circuit can perform its computations, it produces data at output connectors.For safety-critical applications, at design time software circuits are mapped to a time-triggered communication schedule by the off-line scheduling tool.

Chapter 3

REQUIREMENTS OF AN INTEGRATED ARCHITECTURE

Ultra-dependable systems are deployed in applications where the loss of the computer system results in catastrophic consequences. Examples of ultra-dependable systems are X-by-wire applications in the automotive or avionic domain, where a real-time computer system is designed to replace conventional mechanical or hydraulic components. New generations of civil airliners (Airbus A320, A330, A340, Boeing 777) exploit fly-by-wire control by the interposition of the flight control computer between the pilot's commands and the control surface actuators [Collinson, 1999]. In the automotive industry, complete drive-by-wire systems without mechanical backup for braking, steering, and higher-level driver-assisting functions will replace the existing fail-safe systems in cars [Isermann et al., 2002].

The reliability requirements for the controlling computer systems in X-by-wire applications are extremely high. In general, one demands a level of safety that is higher or equal to the level of safety of the systems that are replaced. In these ultra-dependable applications, a maximum failure rate of 10^{-9} critical failures per hour is demanded [Suri et al., 1995]. Today's technology does not support the manufacturing of electronic devices with failure rates low enough to meet these reliability requirements. Since component failure rates are usually in the order of 10^{-5} to 10^{-6} (e.g., [Pauli et al., 1998] uses a large statistical basis and reports 100 to 500 failures out of 1 Million ECUs in 10 years), ultra-dependable applications require the system as a whole to be more reliable than any one of its components. This can only be achieved by utilizing fault-tolerant strategies that enable the continued operation of the system in the presence of component failures [Butler et al., 1991].

Since systems can only be tested to reliability in the order of 10^{-4} failures/hour, a combination of experimental evidence and formal reasoning using a reliability model is needed to construct the safety argument. The safety argument is a set of arguments in order to convince experts in the field that the provided system as a whole is safe to deploy in a given environment.

The justification for building ultra-reliable systems from replicated resources rests on an assumption of failure independence among redundant units. For this reason, the independence of fault containment regions is of critical importance. Thus, any dependence of fault containment regions must be reflected in the dependability model. If complex systems are constructed from components with interdependencies, the reliability model can become extremely complex and the analysis intractable [Butler et al., 1991].

One can distinguish two classes of systems for ultra-dependable applications, namely *federated* and *integrated systems*. These two classes of systems differ in the allocation of functions to the available computer systems. In a federated system, each major function (e.g., autopilot in avionic system or brake-by-wire in automotive system) has its own dedicated computer system with internal redundancy, while an integrated system is characterized by the integration of multiple functions within a single distributed computer system. Federated systems have been preferred for ultra-dependable applications due to the natural separation of application functions, which facilitates fault-isolation and complexity management. Integrated systems, on the other hand, permit an optimal interplay of application functions and improvements with respect to user interfaces. In addition, integrated systems promise massive cost savings through the reduction of resource duplication, reliability improvements with respect to wiring and connectors, and overcome limitations for spare components and redundancy management:

Reduced Resource Consumption. In contrast to federated systems, which require a dedicated computer system for each function, integrated systems permit the multiplexing of hardware resources (e.g., network, node computers) among different functions. In the automotive area, present day modern luxury cars contain almost a hundred computer nodes. For example, the BMW 7 series cars contain up to 70 Electronic Control Units (ECUs) [Deicke, 2002]. The distributed ECUs are interconnected via communication networks with different protocols (e.g., LIN [Audi AG et al., 1999], CAN [Bosch, 1991], MOST [MOST Cooperation, 2002]), physical layers, bandwidths (10 kbps–500 kbps), and dependability requirements. However, this trend of increasing the number of ECUs is coming to its limits, because systems are becoming too complex and too costly with the current practice of having each ECU dedicated to a single function.

Reliability Improvements due to Reductions of Wiring and Connectors. By tackling the "1 Function – 1 ECU" problem, the reduction in the overall number of ECUs also leads to increased reliability by minimizing the number of connectors and wires. Field data from automotive environments has shown that more than 30% of electrical failures are attributed to connector problems [Swingler and McBride, 1999].

Quality of Control. In contrast to federated systems, integrated systems permit a tactic coordination of tightly coupled control activities. In federated systems, control variables that are tightly coupled in the controlled object are often managed by different functions located in separate computer systems. For example, in most transport aircraft, autopilot and autothrottles have been designed as totally independent systems. The missing coordination has lead to interference between autothrottle speed control and autopilot flight path control, making the overall system not only potentially uncomfortable, but also extremely wasteful of fuel [Rushby, 1999a; Wallace, 1994, chap. 6-3].

Homogeneous Computer Systems. Integrated systems enforce platform homogeneity, thus facilitating reusability and platform hardware. Current federated systems, on the other hand, typically use a variety of different platforms (i.e. different hardware, operating systems, application programming interfaces). There is high cost associated with developing and certifying software to run on this multitude of platforms. A typical example is the H009 bus of the F15 fighter plane. This bus is only used by a few vendors and only deployed with the F15 fighter plane [Lowery et al., 2001].

As a consequence, there is the desire to allow multiple functions to share common fault-tolerant computing resources. In the aerospace domain, this design concept is referred to as Integrated Modular Avionics (IMA) [ARINC 651, 1991]. We denote an architecture that provides a framework for the design of such an integrated computer systems as an *integrated architecture*. An integrated architecture offers to the application generic mechanisms, which provide the foundation for an integration of different functions within a single distributed computer system. An example of such a mechanism is error containment for restoring the exterior error propagation barriers of federated systems. Since a federated system employs separate computer systems, a computer system for a particular function remains functional despite the failure of other computer systems and their respective functions.

3.1 Integration Directions

An integrated architecture supports the integration of multiple functions via common shared resources. An integrated architecture should also facilitate the coexistence of functions belonging to different levels of criticality without introducing potential error propagation. In addition, an integrated architecture has to assist in the reuse of legacy subsystems to allow an incremental evolution of a system.

Functional Integration

An integrated architecture provides a framework for distributed systems, in which different functions coordinate to achieve a collective purpose. Although functions can be located at physically separated components, the tight coupling between functions allows the provision of higher-level management functions that ensure a coordination of individual functions to achieve a higher quality of control (e.g., flight control and power control in an aircraft [Wallace, 1994]).

In addition, functional integration offers the potential for a linkage of functions in order to construct simpler and more intuitive user interfaces. While federated architectures enforce the structuring of the user interface in accordance to the layout of the underlying computer system, integrated architectures allow user interface functions to be organized in order to minimize complexity for the operator.

Physical Integration

By integrating multiple functions on a single, shared, fault-tolerant computer system, the distributed computer system becomes a shared resource for several functions. The shared use of standard components and networks lowers resource duplication and the overall number of components and physical networks. Consequently, an integrated architecture can facilitate the reduction of production cost, spares requirements, weight, and volume of embedded computer systems.

In an integrated system, spare components need not be bound to functions, but can be allocated to functions as required. The resulting global resource pool allows normal operation to continue as long as the total number of non-faulty components is sufficient to provide the required level of replication to each function. This increases safety for a given number of redundant components and allows to defer maintenance activities to be scheduled at a convenient time.

It is possible to provide either a *coarse-grained* or a *fine-grained* resource sharing between functions. A coarse-grained physical integration performs resource sharing of a distributed system by dedicating each component to a single function. In a fine-grained integration, a component is shared among multiple functions, possibly with different levels of criticality.

Coarse-Grained Physical Integration: One Component – One Function

In case of a coarse-grained physical integration, each component is dedicated to a single function. Note that the adverse implication does, in general, not apply. For fault-tolerance purposes, a particular function can be allocated to multiple components in order to ensure that replicas of a component are in different FCRs.

Compared to a federated architecture, functions can be subdivided differently and coupled more tightly. For example, a particular function can provide common services to several other functions, which depend on these service in order to be able to offer their own services.

A major strength of dedicating a component exclusively to a single function is that different functions can be assumed to be independently affected by the immediate impact of a hardware fault. As described in [Kopetz, 2003] a component (i.e. an entire node computer constituting a hardware/software unit) represents a reasonable FCR, because computations within a component depend on shared common resources (e.g., computing hardware, power supply, timing source, physical space).

Nevertheless, error containment mechanisms must prevent the propagation of the consequences of a fault, the error between components. A physically integrated system does not offer the natural barriers of a federated architecture, but requires explicit mechanisms as part of the architecture to prevent error propagation.

Fine-Grained Physical Integration: One Component – Multiple Functions

A more fine grained solution to physical integration is the exploitation of a component for multiple functions. In case a single function does not fully occupy the resources of a component, this approach can yield a better resource utilization, thereby offering the potential for an additional reduction in the number of components.

Since multiple functions within a component are likely to be jointly affected by a hardware fault that hits common resources of the component, fault-tolerance through replication requires the redundant computations of a safety-critical function to be performed at different components. In a fine-grained physically integrated system, the dependability model must take into account the higher probability of the correlated failures of multiple replicas of different functions.

Another concern in a system with fine-grained physical integration is independence with respect to software faults. In many cases, the safety argument for the whole system is based on the assumption that the failure of a single function has to be tolerated, as long as other functions operate correctly [Rushby, 1999a, p. 9]. This claim originates from the requirement to tolerate a developmental software fault in any single function. In the absence of software diversity, a replicated developmental software fault can cause the failure of an entire function via a common mode failure in all replicas. In a fine-grained physically integrated system, the developmental software fault will be present in all components executing the function. However, in contrast to hardware faults, we can assume that the boundary of the immediate impact of a software developmental fault is not an entire system component, but only the subsystem of the component executing the function exhibiting this fault. Other functions will be unaffected by the fault, despite the fact that they share components with the faulty function – provided that adequate error containment mechanisms are present in order to prevent the fault to affect correct functions indirectly via an error. This leads to a fundamental requirement for sharing components among multiple functions: inner component error containment between different functions in a component. For components multiplexed among different functions, missing inner component error containment lowers the coverage of the independence assumption of design faults in different functions.

Legacy Software Integration

A legacy system is an information system that resists evolution [Brodie and Stonebreaker, 1995], thereby restricting the opportunities for extensions of the system. Nevertheless, legacy systems often represent major investments and it can be too costly to replace an entire legacy system in a single step. Furthermore, missing experience with new technologies can introduce an additional risk when replacing well-tested legacy applications. In this case, only an evolutionary approach to system architecture leads to a good balance between risk and opportunity. A *managed evolution* occurs by differentially incrementing a system and by successively replacing legacy subsystems with newly developed ones [Koch and Murer, 1999]. The main benefits of this approach are the preservation of the stability of the existing system and the ability to retain experience of engineers with the system. Managed evolution requires the system to be partitioned into manageable components or layers separated by well-specified interfaces. These interfaces must be independent of current technologies and components.

The usual approach for systems that can be developed "from the green lawn" is a top-down approach. Beginning with a requirement specification several iterations of design activities take place towards the actual implementation. However, in the presence of legacy systems a bottom-up approach is better suited for integrating existing components. Hence, for a system being composed of both legacy subsystems and newly developed subsystems, a combination of top-down and bottom-up approaches is required.

An integrated architecture that supports the combination of top-down and bottom-up approaches requires a connecting layer in between [Koch and Murer, 1999]. The establishment of such a connecting layer represents a meeting-in-the-middle design process, where successive refinements of specifications meet with abstractions of potential implementations. In the context of platform-based design [Sangiovanni-Vincentelli, 2002], this layer is described via a system platform, which hides lower-level details but lets through enough information about the lower abstraction level to permit design space exploration and to reason about properties (e.g., temporal) of the final implementation.

An integrated architecture can provide such a connecting layer. Since most legacy applications were designed without considerations of future reuse, the integrated architecture must reestablish the interface of the platform for which a legacy application has been developed. A possible approach for constructing the connecting layer is to distinguish between a set of basic services, which are common to all applications, and a higher layer of services that maps the interfaces expected by legacy applications to the basic services.

An example for such a two layer approach in the avionic domain is described in [Younis et al., 2000]. This work distinguishes between a *system executive* and an *application executive*. The system executive provides general services for resource management based on pre-computed static timetables. The application executive provides the service interface expected by legacy software, namely the API of a particular operating system.

Mixed-Criticality Integration

In federated computer systems, functions of a given criticality level are supported by dedicated hardware with no electrical or electronic connections between components of different criticality levels. As part of the functional and physical integration, it is also desirable to integrate subsystems with different levels of criticality.

A fundamental requirement for such integrated mixed-criticality architectures is the provision of effective error containment mechanisms. Otherwise all functions must be assured and certified to the highest criticality level of a function in the computer system (e.g., level A in ARINC DO-178B [RTCA, 1992]).

On the other hand, effective error containment mechanisms allow functions to be subdivided into subsystems with different levels of criticality. Each subsystem can then be individually certified to the appropriate level of criticality. This modular certification as described in [Rushby, 2001c] allows to reduce cost and to focus assurance effort on the most critical parts of a function.

3.2   Required Properties

This section describes properties required in an integrated architecture for ultra-dependable systems that aims at the integration of different functions on top of a single distributed computing platform. These properties include error containment, temporal predictability, certification support, and composability.

Error Containment

A fundamental requirement for obtaining the benefits of integrated architectures as described in the previous section is the availability of error containment mechanisms. While federated architectures limit error propagation via a high level of independence between the various loosely-coupled computer systems, an integrated architecture must offer adequate mechanisms to prevent error propagation. Otherwise, a fault in one function can affect other functions via the resulting error, although other functions have not been subject to the original fault.

The four integration strategies (functional, physical, legacy, and mixed-criticality) described in the previous section outline the error containment requirements for an integrated architecture. In case functions of mixed-criticality levels are integrated, the architecture must at least prevent error propagation to functions of higher criticality. When existing application code is reused, it is important to avoid interference between legacy subsystems and newly developed subsystems.

Physical integration involves the need to protect functions that share distributed computing resources. The degree of physical integration determines the required error containment capabilities of the integrated architecture. If the distributed computer system is shared among multiple functions, but every component hosts only a single function, then inter-component error containment is sufficient. In case application code of more than one function is executed in a component, inner-component error containment can prevent fault propagation between different functions in a component (e.g., for a software fault of a single function).

Predictability and Real-Time Response Requirements

Achievement of control stability in real-time applications depends on the completion of activities (like reading of sensor values, performing computations, communication activities, actuator control) in bounded time. Hard real-time systems ensure guaranteed response even in the case of peak load and fault scenarios. Guaranteed response involves assurance of temporal correctness of the design without reference to probabilistic arguments. Guaranteed response requires extensive analysis during the design phase such as an off-line timing and resource analysis [Audsley et al., 1998]. An off-line timing and resource analysis assesses the worst-case behavior of the system in terms of communication delays, computational delays, jitter, end-to-end delays, and temporal interference between different activities.

In hard real-time systems, missed deadlines represent system failures with the potential of consequences as serious as in the case of providing incorrect results. For example, in drive-by-wire applications, the dynamics for steered wheels in closed control loops enforce computer delays of less than 2 ms [Heiner and Thurner, 1998]. Taking the vehicle dynamics into account, a transient outage-time of the steering system must not exceed 50 ms [Heiner and Thurner, 1998]. In the avionic domain, variable-cycle jet engines can blow up if correct control inputs are not applied every 20 to 50 ms [Lala and Harper, 1994].

While control algorithms can be designed to compensate a known delay, delay jitter (i.e. the difference between the maximum and minimum value of delay) brings an additional uncertainty into a control loop that has an adverse effect on the quality of control [Kopetz, 1997]. Delay jitter represents an uncertainty about the instant a real-time entity was observed and can be expressed as an additional error in the value domain. In case of low jitter or a global time base with a good precision, state estimation techniques allow to compensate a known delay between the time of observation and the time of use of a real-time image. State estimation uses a model of a real-time entity to compute the probable state of the real-time entity at a future point in time.

Certification Support

Legislatures and the public have decided that certification agencies – such as the Federal Aviation Administration (FAA) for commercial transport aircraft – must monitor the design of safety-critical applications that are crucial to the preservation of human life. Ultra-dependability as demanded for these applications is orders of magnitude from what can be validated experimentally by using measurements and testing. Therefore, certification of ultra-dependable systems must be based on the life-cycle processes of the development, reviews and analysis of the system, and experience gained with similar systems.

Certification is a significant cost factor in the development of ultra-dependable systems, e.g., in the avionic domain [Hayhurst et al., 1999]. Consequently, there is a need for systems that are designed for validation in order to simplify the certification process. Design for validation [Johnson and Butler, 1992] occurs by devising a complete and accurate reliability model, by avoiding design faults, and by minimizing parameters that have to be measured. The construction of the reliability model has to be based on a detailed understanding of failure modes and fault-tolerance mechanisms. The reliability model must be based on parameters that can be accurately measured, e.g., component failure rates.

In an integrated architecture, the core services (e.g., error containment, communication services) are among the most critical parts of the system, since any design fault in these services is likely to result in correlated failures in multiple functions. *The core algorithms and architectural mechanisms in fault-tolerant systems are single points of failure: they just have to work correctly* [Rushby, 2001c, p. 27]. Consequently, high emphasis should be placed on validating correct functionality of the core services of an integrated architecture, e.g., by employing formal verification techniques.

In the context of certification, another major requirement for integrated architectures is the support for modular certification of a distributed computer system. Modular certification separates the certification of architectural services from applications and aims at independent safety arguments for different functions.

1 **Separating certification of architectural services from certification of applications.** Certification efforts can be reduced significantly by separating the safety arguments relating to the core services provided by the integrated architecture and the applications that build on top of this architecture. The certified core services of the integrated architecture can establish a baseline safety argument for the certification of the overall system [Nicholson et al., 2000].

   A prerequisite for the separation of the certification of architectural services from the certification of applications are clear interfaces between the system platform and applications.

2 **Separating certification of different functions.** For cost reasons, an integrated architecture should allow the independent certification of different functions, instead of considering the system as an indivisible whole in the certification process. The deconstruction of functions into smaller subfunctions with different criticality levels reduces the overall certification efforts and allows to focus on the most critical parts. Furthermore, the separate certification of functions is beneficial, if a function is reused in several different applications. In this case, the safety argument for a function needs to be constructed only once. Ideally, the safety argument is provided by the suppliers along with the application code of the corresponding function. For example, in [Morris et al., 2001] a model for software certification is proposed, in which suppliers offer test certificates in a standard portable form.

In order to construct the safety argument for the overall system, the system integrator has to combine the safety arguments of individual functions and acquire additional evidence, such as results of a formal verification of the core services of the integrated architecture.

For evolving systems the ability to reuse certification evidence during the lifetime of a system is important. Maintaining a safety argument despite the modification or addition of functions is denoted as *incremental certification* [Nicholson et al., 2000]. Incremental certification requires the ability to integrate new functions without the need to recertify the whole system. In [Nicholson et al., 2000] different types of changes in evolving systems are distinguished. These changes range from modifications of a single application to modifications in the services of the underlying platform. In the latter case, i.e. when changes are not contained within a function, an impact analysis as described in [Kelly, 1999] becomes necessary.

Composability

In many engineering disciplines, large systems are built by the constructive integration of well-specified and pre-tested components. The components are characterized by their physical parameters and the services they provide across well-specified interfaces. In a composable architecture, this integration should proceed without unintended side effects. An architecture is *composable* with respect to a specific property, if the property is not refuted by the system integration, once the property has been established at the component level [Kopetz, 1997].

Temporal correctness is an example for such a property. Composability with respect to temporal correctness is denoted as *temporal Composability*. The independence of the temporal behavior of different components helps in managing complexity when reasoning about the temporal behavior of the complete system.

For an architecture to be composable [Kopetz and Obermaisser, 2002], it must adhere to the following four principles with respect to the linking interfaces (LIFs) of components:

1 **Independent Development of Components.** Components can only be designed independently of each other, if the architecture supports the exact specification of all component services provided at the LIFs during architecture design. The interface data structures must be precisely specified in the value and time domain.

2 **Stability of Prior Services.** A component must provide the specified services at its service providing linking interface (SPLIF). The stability-of-prior-service principle ensures that the validated services of a component are not refuted by the integration of the component into a larger system.

3 **Performability of the Communication System.** The integration of a component must not disturb the correct operation of the already integrated components. If network resources are managed dynamically, then it must be ensured that even

at the critical instant, i.e. when all components request the network resources at the same instant, the specified timeliness of all communication requests can be satisfied. Otherwise failures will occur sporadically with a failure rate that is increasing with the number of integrated components.

4 **Replica Determinism.** If fault-tolerance is implemented by the replication of components, then the architecture and the components must support replica determinism [Poledna, 1995]. Replica determinism is a prerequisite for exact voting and also significantly decreases testing efforts.

3.3   Generic Architectural Services

Fundamental services of a distributed real-time system are clock synchronization, error detection, and a predictable fault-tolerant communication service. An integrated system will also require effective error containment capabilities, as it does not offer a federated system's natural barriers against error propagation. In particular, physical integration depends on error containment capabilities to preserve independence of functions, despite sharing a common distributed computer system. Error containment is also a prerequisite for mixed-criticality systems. Otherwise, a less critical function can cause the failure of more critical functions.

In order to facilitate reuse and reduce design complexity, these fundamental services should not be intertwined with application functionality. The separation of architectural services from application functionality corresponds to the concept of platform-based design [Sangiovanni-Vincentelli, 2002]. Platform-based design proposes the introduction of abstraction layers, which facilitate refinements into subsequent abstraction layers in the design flow.

An example for such an abstraction layer is the service interface of an integrated architecture that provides a set of generic architectural services. The existence of an application independent service interface significantly reduces development and recertification efforts in evolving systems that undergo incremental changes in applications and/or platforms. Furthermore, the separation of platform-dependent functionality, such as communication services, from application software improves reusability across different platforms. Applications build on an architectural service interface, which can be established on top of numerous platforms. The specification of the architectural services hides the details of the underlying platform, while providing all information required for ensuring the functional and meta-functional (dependability, timeliness) requirements in the design of a safety-critical real-time application.

In order to maximize the number of platforms and applications that can be covered, the architectural service interface should establish a minimal set of stable basic services. Restricting the number of basic services also eases a thorough validation (e.g., permitting a formal verification), which is crucial for preventing common mode failures as all functions build on the basic services.

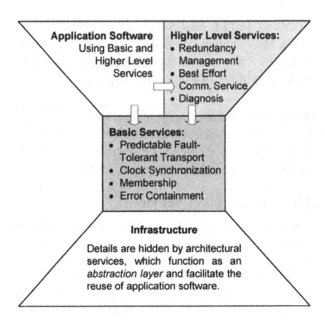

Figure 3.1. Architectural Services

Of course, a minimal set of basic services does not prevent an integrated architecture from offering additional generic services for simplifying application development. However, these additional services should not be intertwined with the basic services for preserving generality and controlling the complexity of the validation process.

Figure 3.1 depicts an example of an integrated architecture, which provides a set of four basic services. This set includes a predictable fault-tolerant message transport, clock synchronization, error containment, and error detection (membership) services. Characteristic for these basic services is a significant level of mutual dependence, e.g., clock synchronization will usually be based on the transport service. In case of a time-triggered communication service, which is becoming commonly accepted for safety-critical applications [Rushby, 2001b], the transport service will also depend on clock synchronization.

In addition to the four basic services, the integrated architecture provides higher-level services that depend on the basic services. While safety-critical applications will rarely be able to do without the functionality of the four basic services, the utility of higher-level services will vary significantly with actual applications. An example for an important higher-level service is redundancy management for hiding replication as part of systematic fault-tolerance from applications. Another useful higher-level service is a best-effort communication service that is tailored to non safety-critical applications and optimized for average performance and resource efficiency.

The remainder of this section will discuss the basic and higher-level services of the integrated architecture depicted in Figure 3.1.

Predictable Fault-Tolerant Message Transport

The purpose of the communication service is the transport of messages from the Communication Network Interface (CNI) of the sender to CNIs of the receivers. Due to the many different and, partially, contradicting requirements, there exists no single model for building a communication service. Well-known tradeoffs are predictability versus flexibility, design for sporadic data vs. periodic data, and resource adequacy versus best-effort strategies [Kopetz, 1995a]. Thus, the chosen communication protocol depends heavily on the requirements of the application.

A fundamental decision in the design of a communication service is the choice between an event-triggered and a time-triggered communication service. As described in Section 2.4, event-triggered communication systems can offer immediate response and excel with respect to flexibility and handling of sporadic messages. Time-triggered communication systems, on the other hand, are superior with respect to predictability, composability, error detection, error containment and handling of periodic message exchanges.

Clock Synchronization

Due to clock drifts, the clock times in an ensemble of clocks will drift apart, if clocks are not periodically resynchronized. Clock synchronization is concerned with bringing the values of clocks in close relation with respect to each other. A measure for the quality of synchronization is the precision. An ensemble of clocks that are synchronized to each other with a specified precision offers a global time. The global time of the ensemble is represented by the local time of each clock, which serves as an approximation of the global time [Kopetz and Ochsenreiter, 1987].

The reasonableness condition [Kopetz, 1997] for a global time base ensures that the synchronization error is bounded to less than one macrogranule. However, due to the synchronization and digitalization error it is impossible to establish the temporal order of occurrences based on their timestamp, if timestamps differ by only a single tick. A solution to this problem is the introduction of a sparse time base [Kopetz, 1992] as described in Section 2.1.

Error Containment Mechanisms

Error containment is achieved by mechanisms that ensure that a failure in one FCR does not propagate to cause a failure in another FCR. These error containment mechanisms are commonly referred to as *partitioning* [Rushby, 1999a]. *Inter-component partitioning* prevents error propagation via the communication system and involves an independent component for monitoring and mediating a component's access to the shared network. *Inner-component partitioning* prevents error propagation between different functions within a component. Without inner-component partitioning, a fault impacting a single function (since the function is a FCR for this fault) can corrupt code or data of other functions within that component via a subsequent error. A faulty function can also affect the ability of other functions to obtain access to shared resources (e.g., CPU). In analogy to inter-component partitioning, inner-component partitioning depends on an independent FCR for error detection and isolation. As the operating system can be assumed to form an independent FCR for software faults, the operating system is capable of performing error detection and isolation in other FCRs (i.e. application tasks) of the component by controlling the memory protection mechanisms and by executing a suitable scheduling strategy.

For both inter- and inner-component partitioning, one can distinguish two types of isolation [Rushby, 1999a]:

1 **Spatial Partitioning:** Spatial partitioning ensures that software in one FCR cannot alter the code or private data of another FCR. Spatial partitioning also prevents a FCR from interfering with control of external devices (e.g., actuators) of other FCRs.

2 **Temporal Partitioning:** Temporal partitioning ensures that a FCR cannot affect the ability of other FCRs to access shared resources, such as the common network or a shared CPU. This includes the temporal behavior of the services provided by resources (latency, jitter, duration of availability during a scheduled access).

Temporal Inter-Component Partitioning

Temporal partitioning at the inter-component level ensures that a function cannot affect the correct temporal behavior of functions in other components. The communication activities of a faulty component via the common network may neither impact the timely exchange of information between correct components, nor the ability of correct components to finish computations before deadlines. For example, a sender suffering a babbling idiot failure must be prevented from denying service to other senders or from overloading its recipients. In case of a push interface for message receptions (as described in Section 2.4), the CPU load generated from interrupts for handling incoming messages can cause a recipient to miss deadlines.

The main mechanism for establishing temporal inter-partitioning is mediating each component's access to the network by some component that will fail independently, i.e. a different FCR. Depending on the communication system paradigm, this mediation is based on a global communication schedule or on a quota system.

- **Time-Triggered Communication Systems:** In a time-triggered system, transmissions are determined by a global schedule, which specifies the global points in times when messages are exchanged. The mediating component need only have an independent copy of the communication schedule and an independent clock. An example for a mediating component is the bus guardian of the Time-Triggered Architecture [Temple, 1998].

- **Event-Triggered Communication Systems:** Building a mediating components in an event-triggered system is complicated by the fact that it is in general impossible to decide whether a communication activity is legitimate without reproducing the computations of the sender. A possibility for limiting the consequences of a faulty component is the provision of a quota scheme, which assigns a maximum share of the communication resources to every component. Based on this information, a mediating component can control the rate of message transmissions of components, blocking transmission attempts that exceed the maximum share. An example for a communication protocol that imposes such a limit on network accesses is Avionics Full Duplex Switched Ethernet (AFDX) [ARINC 664 – Part 7, 2003].

Spatial Inter-Component Partitioning

Spatial inter-component partitioning must ensure that no messages with corrupted data or wrong addresses are delivered. A message with a wrong address or identification – also called a masquerading failure – could cause valid messages of other components to be overwritten at the recipient. Faults occurring at the channel can be detected using CRC checks. For faults that occur within the sender, an unforgeable authentication mechanism is necessary. Depending on the failure assumptions, an authentication mechanism can be implemented with simple signature schemes or cryptographic mechanisms [Goldwasser et al., 1988].

Temporal Inner-Component Partitioning

The primary source of temporal fault propagation within a component is a task, which delays other tasks by holding a shared resource. The most important resource in a component is the shared processor, which can be blocked by a task executing longer than specified. A further source of temporal fault propagation is the use of interrupts. In general, interrupt handling requires processing time at the operating system, even in case no task activation occurs.

The allocation of processor time to tasks is the purpose of the scheduler. In a real-time system, the scheduler must not only ensure that each task obtains a predefined ratio of the processor, but also that execution occurs at the right time and with a high level of temporal predictability. Based on the time when scheduling decision are made, one can distinguish between static and dynamic schedulers. In static scheduling an offline tool creates a schedule, which contains pre-computed scheduling decisions for each point in time. The static temporal control structure created by the offline tool can prevent interference between tasks. The major strengths of static scheduling are predictability and simplicity [Chung and Dietz, 1996].

Dynamic scheduling performs the selection of the task that is to be executed at runtime, e.g., based on task priorities. A major benefit of a dynamic scheduler is the higher flexibility and better support for sporadic tasks [Burns, 1993]. In a partitioned component, a dynamic scheduler should employ a quota system in the scheduling of tasks in order to limit the consequences of a temporal fault in a task.

Spatial Inner-Component Partitioning

The purpose of spatial partitioning within a component is preventing tasks from overwriting data elements or code of other tasks, as well as preventing tasks from interfering in the control of external devices (e.g., sensors, actuators). An obvious solution for establishing spatial partitioning is the use of memory protection mechanisms. In case of memory-mapped I/O, memory protection also ensures non-interference in the control of external devices. Memory protection can occur through hardware mediation, if the processor is equipped with a memory management unit (MMU). Such a processor distinguishes two modes, user and supervisor mode. The operating system runs in supervisor mode and manages MMU tables. For each task, these MMU tables determine the accessible physical memory areas. If the accessible physical memory areas of tasks are kept disjoint, tasks are prevented from manipulating code or data of other tasks, except for dedicated shared memory regions. An analysis of hardware-based memory protection for safety-critical real-time systems can be found in [Bennett and Audsley, 2001]. This work also analyses the consequences with respect to predictability of virtual memory with MMUs of available processors.

Membership Service

In [Cristian, 1991a] the membership problem is defined as the problem of achieving agreement on the identity of all correctly functioning processes of a process group. A process is correct, if its behavior complies with the specification. Otherwise the process is denoted as faulty. For being able to solve the membership problem, a process failure model [Powell, 1992] is required as part of the system assumptions. This model restricts how a faulty process can possibly interact with its environment, e.g., what messages it can send via the communication system.

In the context of integrated architecture, it makes sense to establish membership information for FCRs, since FCRs can be expected to fail independently. Depending on the assumed types of faults, a FCR is either an entire system component or a subsystem within a component (e.g., a task) dedicated to a function.

A service that implements an algorithm for solving the membership problem and offers consistent membership information is called a *membership service*. A membership service simplifies the provision of many application algorithms, since the architecture offers generic error detection capabilities via this service. Applications can rely on the consistency of the membership information and react to detected failures of FCRs as indicated by the membership service.

A membership service also plays an important role for controlling application level fault-tolerance mechanisms that deal with failures of functions. If a function fails – since more FCRs have failed than can be tolerated by the given amount of redundancy – all that an integrated architecture can do is to inform other functions about this condition so they can react accordingly by application level fault-tolerance mechanisms.

Higher-Level Services

The purpose of the higher-level services of the integrated architecture is easing application development by offering generic solutions for common problems in the design of applications. By separating these services from the application functionality, development and certification complexity can be significantly reduced.

Best-Effort Communication Service

In mixed-criticality systems, it can be desirable to refrain from a resource-adequacy policy for cost reasons. When the provision of resources is biased towards average demands, temporal guarantees can only be given probabilistically.

While a time-triggered communication is well-suited for the predictable, fault-tolerant, basic transport service, event-triggered communication can be an effective approach for the best-effort communication service. An integrated architecture with higher-level event-triggered services layered on top of a time-triggered basic communication service will be introduced in Chapter 4.

In [Kopetz, 2001], three fundamental interfaces of a distributed real-time system are identified. The real-time service (RS) interface requires fault-tolerance and stringent temporal guarantees, which corresponds to the properties required at the basic communication service. For the diagnostic and manangement (DM), and the configuration and planning (CP) interfaces, however, a best-effort communication service will usually be sufficient and provide a more resource efficient and cost effective solution. The DM interface enables a maintenance engineer to access component internals in order to set component parameters and to retrieve diagnostic information about detected malfunctions, e.g., from on-board diagnostics in automotive systems [Godavarty et al., 2000]. Hence, activities at the DM interface are inherently event-triggered, because an engineer decides dynamically which data elements are relevant for the maintenance activities. The CP interface is used to connect a component to other components of the system.

Redundancy Management

A function can be implemented by a group of redundant, independent components in order to ensure that the function remains available despite the occurrence of component failures. If the number and types of component failures are covered by the underlying failure mode assumptions, the group will mask failures of its members [Cristian, 1991b].

A common approach for masking component failures is N-modular redundancy (NMR)[Randell et al., 1978; Avizienis, 1975; Lee and Anderson, 1990]. N replicas receive the same requests and provide the same service. The output of all replicas is provided to a voting mechanism, which selects one of the results (e.g., based on majority) or transforms the results to a single one (average voter). The most frequently used N-modular configuration is triple-modular redundancy (TMR). By employing three components and a voter, a single consistent value failure in one of the constituting components can be tolerated.

The major strength of group masking is the ability to handle component failures systematically at the architecture level, i.e. transparently to the application. The purpose of the redundancy management services of the architecture is the provision of mechanisms required for managing the redundant groups of replicas in a way that masks component failures and makes the group functionally indistinguishable from a single replica.

Diagnosis

While the membership service yields diagnostic information as a basic architectural service that enables a coordinated reaction to faults, an integrated architecture should also provide generic diagnostic services aimed at easing maintenance activities. A simple approach would be the accumulation of membership information over time to provide a maintenance engineer with the data to decide whether a component should be replaced. However, an accurate condition assessment of components will in general require information exceeding the binary classification offered by a membership service. For electronic components, the increase of transient failures is a suitable indicator for wear out [Bondavalli et al., 1997]. Suitable condition assessment techniques [Wetzer et al., 2000] are also the key for advanced maintenance strategies like condition-based maintenance. Condition-based maintenance is increasingly replacing conventional time based maintenance, as it reduces costs and improves reliability and systems performance [Teal and Sorensen, 2001].

Ideally, maintenance oriented diagnostic services should include functions for recording and analyzing every anomaly in the system in order to gain an effective assessment of component conditions. Diagnosis should consider anomalies, even if they are masked by fault-tolerance mechanisms and therefore rendered transparent to applications. For example, a triple-modular-redundancy system can provide information about a disagreeing processor in addition to masking the effects of faults.

A fundamental prerequisite for a maintenance oriented diagnostic service are the error containment capabilities of the architecture, because the absence of error containment mechanisms causes the inability to identify the locations of failures. The resulting trouble-not-identified phenomenon [Thomas et al., 2002] is currently a prevalent problem, as it leads to the replacement of correct components (e.g., in the automotive industry).

Chapter 4

INTEGRATED SYSTEM ARCHITECTURE FOR EVENT-TRIGGERED AND TIME-TRIGGERED CONTROL PARADIGMS

This chapter presents a distributed system architecture that integrates the event-triggered and time-triggered control paradigms. The system architecture aims at the four integration directions (physical, functional, mixed-criticality, legacy) of an integrated architecture, with emphasis on the reuse of legacy system and the coexistence of applications with mixed-criticality levels. Time-triggered services provide the foundation for safety-critical functions. Event-triggered services support legacy applications and functions with lower criticality levels. The first part of this chapter describes the underlying synchrony model and relates the proposed integrated system architecture to the well-studied models of synchronous and asynchronous systems. Subsequently, we present the services of the integrated system architecture. We use fundamental services of a time-triggered architecture (time-triggered transport, clock synchronization, error containment, and membership) as the architecture's basic services. On top of the basic services, we construct higher-level services aiming at mixed-criticality and legacy system integration. We establish event-triggered communication channels on top of the time-triggered transport protocol and compose multiple event-triggered communication channels into virtual networks. Gateways interconnect virtual networks with other virtual networks and with physical networks.

In the second part of this chapter, we model the component level via two distinct subsystems. The time-triggered subsystem is fully synchronous and designed for safety-critical functions. The event-triggered subsystem complies with the quasi-synchronous model and permits probabilistic bounds for communication and computational delays. Hence, the event-triggered subsystem allows a more cost effective and resource efficient solution for non-safety critical functions.

The last part of this chapter specifies the fault hypothesis of the integrated system architecture and describes the construction of error detection mechanisms and an event-triggered membership service. The error detection mechanism must take the additional failure modes of the event-triggered subsystem into account, which originate from probabilistic temporal specifications. The event-triggered membership service is based on failure detectors in the time-triggered subsystem, which monitor the behavior of the event-triggered subsystem and provide local views of the operational state of tasks in event-triggered subsystems. A global consistent membership vector is established by exchanging local views via the synchronous communication channel of the time-triggered subsystem and performing majority voting.

4.1   Synchrony Model

Figure 4.1 depicts the synchrony model for the architecture integrating event-triggered and time-triggered subsystems. The architecture is based on the timing failure detection model introduced by Veríssimo et al. in [Almeida and Verissimo, 1998]. We extend this model by mapping the subsystems with the different degrees of synchrony to the event-triggered and time-triggered control paradigms.

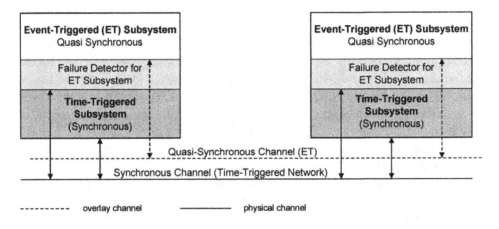

Figure 4.1.   Quasi-Synchronous and Synchronous Subsystems

In the proposed system model, components contain two subsystems: an event-triggered subsystem and a time-triggered subsystem. The time-triggered subsystems of components are linked by a time-triggered communication system. The time-triggered subsystems of components in combination with the time-triggered communication system form the *time-triggered subsystem* (of the overall system). The time-triggered communication system establishes a synchronous communication channel with known and bounded communication latencies. In addition, the time-triggered subsystems exhibits bounded and known computational latencies and the drift rates of local clocks are bounded and known. Consequently, the time-triggered subsystem complies to the synchronous system model (as defined in Section 2.3).

The event-triggered subsystems of components are linked by an event-triggered communication system. The event-triggered subsystems of components in combination with the event-triggered communication system form the *event-triggered subsystem* (of the overall system). As depicted in Figure 4.1, the event-triggered subsystem lies on top of the time-triggered subsystem. For the event-triggered subsystem, computational and communication latencies are probabilistically bounded. Hence, the event-triggered subsystem adheres to the quasi-synchronous system model.

The motivation for the integration of two subsystems with different degrees of synchrony is as follows:

- **Legacy Applications:** Many legacy applications have been part of event-triggered systems, in which defining conditions of synchrony are fulfilled only probabilistically. Quasi-synchronism is therefore a suitable model for many legacy applications and their underlying architectures. For example, event-based computational models can complicate the determination of worst-case computational latencies, since the progress of computations depends on the occurrence of events. Likewise, the temporal behavior of event occurrences determines the transmission latencies of an event-triggered communication system. An event-triggered communication system resolves contention between multiple senders by delaying all but a single message transmission, thereby causing load-dependent transmission latencies.

  An integrated architecture that offers the services of the platform, for which a particular class of legacy applications has been developed, allows to reuse these legacy applications without redevelopment and revalidation efforts. The quasi-synchronous subsystem aims at the construction of such an execution environment for legacy applications by emulating the communication and operating system services of a legacy platform.

  Despite the existence of an underlying synchronous subsystem, the integrated legacy applications continue to exhibit quasi-synchronism, if the load patterns and computational latencies of the legacy applications are not deterministically known.

- **Non Safety-Critical Applications:** For non-safety critical applications, probabilistic temporal guarantees are often accepted for economic reasons, in favor of lower resource consumption. The quasi-synchronous subsystem offers generic services tailored to the requirements of these applications. For example, error detection handles the additional failure modes, such as performance failures, introduced through probabilistic service specifications. The communication service can be optimized for average performance and resource efficiency. If the correlation between the resource usages of different applications is known, resources can be multiplexed between different applications, while providing probabilistic guarantees for communication latencies and sufficiency of buffering capacities.

The grouping of non safety-critical applications that are likely to exhibit occasional timing failures also eases the ability to isolate failures from applications with higher levels of criticality.

- **Provision of Services to the Quasi-Synchronous Subsystem that Require Stronger Synchrony:** The quasi-synchronous subsystem can benefit from the existence of the underlying synchronous subsystem, since the synchronous subsystem supports deterministic solutions to important problems, such as the consensus problem. In the proposed system architecture, the synchronous subsystem performs error detection for the quasi-synchronous subsystem via local failure detectors (e.g., timing failure detection) and agreement to achieve consistent membership information. In addition, the error detection mechanisms of the synchronous subsystem are the basis for error containment between FCRs in quasi-synchronous subsystems.

Synchronous Time-Triggered Subsystem

The time-triggered subsystem of the presented system architecture is synchronous and satisfies the defining conditions of synchrony (see Section 2.3). In particular, the time-triggered subsystem possesses known and bounded latencies for computational and communication activities of correct components. The existence of these bounds simplifies the development of fault-tolerant systems, because correct components executing a common algorithm can use the passage of time to predict each others' progress.

In addition to the compliance with the synchronous model, the time-triggered subsystem derives all control signals from the progression of the synchronized global time base. The underlying computational model of this subsystem is the time-triggered model of computation. A time-triggered communication protocol as described in Section 2.4 comprises the synchronous communication channel and links the time-triggered subsystems of components. Messages are globally and statically scheduled and transmitted at a priori specified points in time. The bounded and known communication latencies can be guaranteed independently from the behavior of host applications.

Quasi-Synchronous Event-Triggered Subsystem

The event-triggered subsystem is a delimited, well-defined part of the overall system, which complies to the quasi-synchronous model. An event-triggered communication system as described in Section 2.4 establishes a quasi-synchronous communication channel for interconnecting the event-triggered subsystems of components. Since the network load is not completely controlled, the quasi-synchronous communication channel exhibits a non-zero probability for violations of bounds on communication latencies. Nevertheless, the quasi-synchronous communication channel can offer a flexible and resource efficient communication service that allows applications to initiate communication activities on-demand in order to react to significant events. The event-triggered subsystem supports an event-based computational model.

4.2 Architecture

This section describes the services of the proposed integrated system architecture. This system architecture has been designed to meet the requirements for an integrated architecture for safety-critical systems presented in Chapter 3. The integrated system architecture is based on a time-triggered architecture, the services of which serve as the foundation for applications and higher-level architectural services. The time-triggered architectural services are therefore the basic services of the integrated architecture, while higher-level event-triggered architectural services build on top of the time-triggered services.

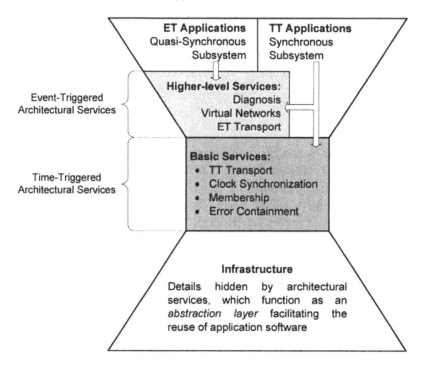

Figure 4.2. Integrated System Architecture

Figure 4.2 shows the resulting waist-line system architecture. This architecture supports two subsystems with different degrees of synchrony. The applications in the quasi-synchronous subsystem exploit the event-triggered architectural services. The applications in the synchronous subsystem can access the time-triggered architectural services directly or exploit the event-triggered architectural services for non-critical communication activities, such as diagnosis.

Basic Services

The time-triggered basic services are centric to the architecture, since higher-level services build on top of these basic services. These basic services include a time-triggered transport service, clock synchronization, membership and error containment.

1 **Time-Triggered Transport of Messages:** The time-triggered transport service is offered by a time-triggered communication service as described in Section 2.4. This transport service is available via the temporal firewall interface, which eliminates control error propagation by design and minimizes coupling between components.

2 **Fault-Tolerant Clock Synchronization:** Due to clock drifts, the clock times in an ensemble of clocks will drift apart, if clocks are not periodically resynchronized. Clock synchronization is concerned with bringing the values of clocks in close relation with respect to each other. The clock synchronization is a fundamental service in a time-triggered system, since all activities are controlled by the progression of time.

3 **Membership Service:** The membership service provides consistent information about the operational state (correct or faulty) of nodes. The membership service is based on the a priori knowledge about the points in time of the time-triggered message exchanges. In a time-triggered system the periodic message send times are the membership points of the sender [Kopetz, 1997]. Every receiver knows a priori when a message of a sender is supposed to arrive, and interprets the arrival of the message as a life sign at the membership point of the sender. From the arrival of the expected messages at two consecutive membership points, it can be concluded that a node was operational during the interval delimited by these membership points.

4 **Error Containment:** Although a fault containment region (FCR) can demarcate the immediate impact of a fault, fault effects manifested as erroneous data can propagate across FCR boundaries. For this reason, the system must also provide error containment [Lala and Harper, 1994]. To avoid error propagation by the flow of erroneous messages the error detection mechanisms must be part of different FCRs than the message sender. Otherwise, the error detection service can be affected by the same fault that caused the message failure.

Event-Triggered Transport Service

The event-triggered transport service establishes event-triggered communication channels (ETCCs) in order to support on-demand communication activities, i.e. message exchanges as a response to significant event occurrences. An ETCC is a unidirectional interface for the exchange of event messages between nodes of a distributed computer system. An ETCC exhibits a one-to-many communication relationship and maps to exactly one service providing linking interface (SPLIF) and n service requesting linking interfaces (SRLIFs). The node with the SPLIF connected to the ETCC acts as sender (producer) and exclusively generates messages for the ETCC. These messages are received by all nodes with a service requesting linking interface (SRLIF) connected to the ETCC (see Figure 4.3). The transport

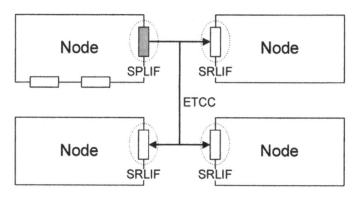

Figure 4.3. Interconnection of Nodes Through an Event-Triggered Communication Channel

of the event messages occurs via the underlying time-triggered transport protocol. In the Time Division Multiple Access (TDMA) scheme, a communication slot of the sender node is assigned to the ETCC.

Both the sender and the receivers operate event-triggered. The host application in the sender determines the points in time when message transmission requests are being made. Accordingly, the host applications at the receiver's side decide upon the points in time for fetching received messages from the communication system.

Control and Data Flow between Nodes

If a system uses event information, every event is significant in order to maintain state synchronization between sender and receiver. To ensure an exactly-once processing of data elements containing event information, data items are buffered at the interface and removed on reading. Due to finite buffer capacities, the consumer must remove data items from the buffer to allow the producer to place additional data items into the buffer. Most event-triggered systems apply *composite interfaces* for avoiding buffer overflows. A control signal informs the producer about the consumer's ability to receive a further data element, thereby applying explicit flow control. In such a communication relationship a unidirectional data flow involves a bi-directional control flow.

An ETCC provides an *elementary interface* [Kopetz, 1999a]. The information flow and the interface control flow are both unidirectional. The information producing subsystem can perform its information dissemination function without depending on any control signals from the information consuming subsystem. As described in [Kopetz, 1999a] an elementary interface is more robust and easier to validate, analyze and understand than a composite interface. An ETCC acts as an error-propagation boundary by being an elementary interface. In a composite interface an error in the consuming subsystem propagates back into the producing subsystem and affects its operations. At the level of the communication system an elementary interface prevents such an error propagation from the consumer to the producer. The ETCC's buffer management functionality is determined by the unidirectional control flow. A buffer overflow – e.g., due to an imbalance of message production and consumption rates – does not block the sender, but results in a message omission failure. In order to preserve the exactly-once semantics for processing data elements, implicit flow control through design time restrictions is necessary. The design time restrictions can be established by specifying bounds for the maximum production rate of the sender and the minimum consumption rates of receivers. If the events that trigger message transmissions are generated internally by a component, they are within the sphere of control of the computer system. Therefore, these bounds can form inputs for the component design phase. In case the message transmissions result from events occurring in the natural environment, control lies outside the sphere of control of the computer system. An analysis of the natural environment is the basis for determining the rates of these event occurrences. Such rates are an input for dimensioning the bandwidth and buffer capacities in ETCCs during architecture design.

The establishment of deterministic bounds must investigate the worst-case arrival rates of events, e.g., considering the case that all events occur simultaneously. A probabilistic approach is an alternative, if it is undesirable or too costly to specify deterministic bounds for consumption or production rates. For this purpose, queuing theory allows to construct a mathematical model of the buffering behavior of the ETCC [Obermaisser, 2003b]. Important applications of such a queuing theoretical model for an ETCCs are:

1 **Probabilistic Bounds for Transmission Latencies.** The knowledge about message interarrival and service time distributions is the basis for the establishment of probabilistic bounds for the transmission latencies of an ETCC. In combination with real-time queuing theory approaches, such as [Lehoczky, 1996], it is possible to satisfy explicit timing requirements probabilistically.

2 **Dimensioning of Queues.** Messages that are received via an ETCC are buffered in incoming message queues, which represent the event-triggered SRLIF. Queu-

ing theory supports the calculation of probabilities for the accumulation of a certain number of a messages in these incoming message queues.

3 **Multiplexing of ETCCs.** Queuing theory allows to reason about transmission latencies and queuing capacities in case an ETCC is multiplexed among different applications within a component.

A fundamental limit to these probabilistic approaches is the completeness of the knowledge about the *probability distributions* of event occurrences and the *correlation* between events. Incomplete knowledge limits the ability to determine the probability for timing and omission failures due to event overloads.

Another problem originates from incomplete knowledge of *processing delays.* In case the knowledge about processing delays is also probabilistic (e.g., probabilistic worst-case execution times as described in [Bernat et al., 2002]), the corresponding execution models should be integrated into the probabilistic model of the communication system.

Control and Data Flow between Applications and Comm. Service

The producing subsystem of an ETCC deposits its output information into an outgoing event queue according to the information push paradigm, while the consuming subsystem must pull received information out of its incoming event queue. The information push model [DeLine, 1999] presumes that the sender presses the information on the receiver. This model is ideal for the sender, because the sender can determine the points in time for passing outgoing information to the communication system. The information pull model is ideal for the receiver, since tasks of the receiver will not be interrupted by an incoming message.

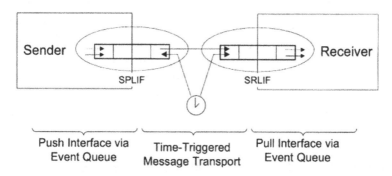

Figure 4.4.   Event-Triggered Communication Channel: Information and Control Flow

The outgoing event queue at the producer corresponds to the component's SPLIF, the incoming event queue at the consumer to the SRLIF. As shown in Figure 4.4 the transport of the information is realized by a time-triggered communication system that derives its control signals autonomously from the progression of time.

Mapping of an ETCC to the Time-Triggered Transport Service

Applications can exploit the event-triggered transport service by placing event messages into outgoing message queues and by consuming received event messages from incoming message queues. The message transmission requests of a node will result in a sequential stream of event messages that forms the input to an ETCC. The insertion of inactivity messages can preserve the assumption of a coherent message stream during time intervals, in which applications do not produce messages.

The event-triggered transport service is a higher-level service that must be mapped to the basic time-triggered services of the architecture. An effective approach for this mapping is the use of a packet service that builds on top of the time-triggered transport protocol. This approach does not require any modification to the basic services, such as the time-triggered communication protocol. The packet service can use a fraction of a node's slot in the time-triggered communication schedule for establishing an ETCC. Thereby, the ETCC of a node maps to a dedicated slot of the time-triggered communication schedule. In every node, the packet service performs a fragmentation of outgoing messages into packets. These packets are placed in the node's communication slot dedicated to event-triggered communication. Furthermore, the packet service fuses received packets into event messages and offers these messages to the application via incoming event message queues.

Virtual Networks

A *virtual network* is an overlay network that is established on top of a physical network. In the integrated system architecture, we provide event-triggered virtual networks and employ a time-triggered backbone as the physical network.

In general, a receiver will require messages from more than a single sender and it may also send messages via an event-triggered communication channel of its own. More general communication relationships, i.e. many-to-many instead of one-to-many relationships, are enabled through the composition of ETCCs into virtual networks. A virtual network enables each node with an event-triggered subsystem to disseminate a message that is being received by all other nodes with an event-triggered subsystem.

Composition of Event-Triggered Communication Channels into a Virtual Network

Virtual networks result from the composition of ETCCs. A virtual network, which interconnects n nodes acting as senders, employs at least n ETCCs. In case a node hosts more than one application subsystem that accesses the virtual network, the application subsystems can either share a single ETCC (node local contention) or employ separate ETCCs (contentionless) for every application subsystem. Since every ETCC maps to a slot in the time-triggered communication schedule, a virtual network for n senders uses n communication slots.

An example for the composition of ETCCs into a virtual network and the corresponding communication behavior on the underlying time-triggered network are depicted in Figure 4.5. This example assumes a single ETCC per node, i.e. either a single application subsystem per node or an ETCC that is shared between multiple application subsystems.

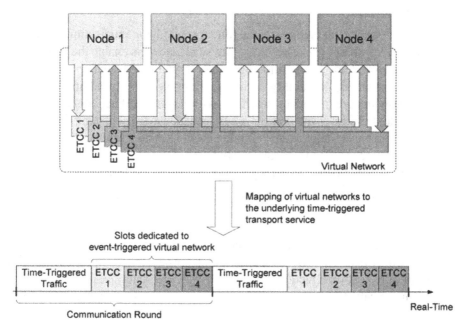

Figure 4.5. Composition of Event-Triggered Communication Channels into a Virtual Network

Virtual Network for Legacy Applications

Virtual networks that emulate existing event-triggered networks enable the integrated system architecture to provide the communication services expected by event-triggered legacy applications. The emulation of an existing event-triggered communication system consists of two parts, namely an emulation of the event-triggered network and an emulation of the legacy communication controller. *Protocol emulation* incorporates the behavior of the emulated network and establishes significant properties of the event-triggered communication protocol, such as a specific message ordering. The emulation of the *legacy communication controller* includes the provision of the controller's programming interface, i.e. the CNI expected by event-triggered applications. The controller emulation must also incorporate the services of the emulated communication controller, such as message filtering, buffer management, flow control, error detection, and error recovery.

Gateway Services

Gateways are required for the coupling of different (sub-)networks. A gateway serves two main purposes, namely to bridge local limitations and to overcome architectural discrepancies of subnetworks in heterogeneous communication systems [Johannsen et al., 1988]. The integrated system architecture distinguishes between physical and logical gateways.

Physical Gateways

A *physical gateway* interconnects the time-triggered communication service or a virtual network with a physical network. Physical gateways enable the construction of multi-cluster systems for partitioning a large system into smaller subnetworks, e.g., in order to obtain scalability or manage complexity. In addition, physical gateways allow to access fieldbus networks with sensors and actuators.

In the context of legacy integration, physical gateways also extend the potential for reusability of legacy applications. While virtual networks support the integration of existing software into components of a time-triggered system, physical gateways facilitate the reuse of complete legacy computer clusters – legacy components interconnected by a dedicated network.

Logical Gateways

A *logical gateway* is a generic architectural service offering gateway functionality between virtual networks. An important purpose of logical gateways is to preserve the ability for interactions across well-specified interfaces, while encapsulating communication of different functions in separate virtual networks. The use of multiple virtual networks instead of a single, shared virtual networks for all functions simplifies the reasoning about the temporal behavior of message exchanges – since an analysis includes fewer sender applications. Furthermore, separate virtual networks enable error containment through generic architectural services. The architecture can ensure the encapsulation of different virtual networks by preventing an overload in one virtual network from having an adverse effect on a second virtual network.

Another application of logical gateways is the integration of multi-cluster legacy systems. The integrated architecture can provide a dedicated virtual network for each cluster of the legacy system, interconnecting these virtual networks via logical gateways that replace the physical gateways of the legacy system.

Besides filtering, protocol conversions, and support for different traffic types, logical gateways offer the following benefits:

- **Generic Architectural Service:** Generic services can be used in a variety of different applications, thereby reducing development time and focusing the development on application functionality.

- **Reuse:** Logical gateways facilitate reuse through the definition of stable interfaces towards applications.

- **Cost reduction:** A primary motivation for the deployment of virtual networks is the reduction of hardware costs. Logical gateways can be fully implemented in software, i.e. without needing dedicated hardware, wiring, and connectors.

- **Increased Dependability:** Minimizing of wiring and the number of connectors reduces potential sources for hardware faults, thereby increasing reliability.

- **Flexibility:** Logical gateways offer high flexibility in the design and implementation of the system structure. Thus, different virtual network topologies can easily be evaluated by changing the system structure.

- **Portability:** Logical gateways can be established on different hardware platforms. This enables the reuse of the gateway services along with corresponding applications, independently from the actual hardware.

- **Dynamic Reconfiguration:** By reallocating logical gateways in the system, an adaption to changing situations is possible. Incremental upgrades of the system can be performed by shifting the borders of the virtual networks. Thus, an evolutionary change rather than reengineering the system in a single step is made possible [Swanson, 1998].

- **Migration:** Migration is supported by moving gateway functionality between components.

Diagnostic Services

The diagnostic services of the proposed system architecture establish consistent global membership information for the quasi-synchronous event-triggered subsystems of components. This event-triggered membership is based on the basic membership service of the architecture. In addition, components perform local error detection. The global consistent membership vector is reached by exchanging these local views and by agreeing on a consistent view.

We will describe the diagnostic services in Section 4.5 after the fault hypothesis of the proposed system architecture has been specified.

4.3 Component Level

At the component level, our system architecture employs a second level communication controller for mapping the state message interface of the time-triggered communication system to the event-triggered LIF. Applications in the event-triggered subsystem of a component exploit the event-triggered virtual network provided by the second level communication controller, whereas applications in the time-triggered subsystem can access the state message interface of the time-triggered communication system directly.

Component Subsystems

A component, which is depicted in Figure 4.6, runs two execution environments in parallel: an environment for applications performing event-triggered communication (component's event-triggered subsystem), and an environment for applications that exploit the time-triggered communication service directly (component's time-triggered subsystem). The host computer is shared between the two types of applications. In this context the terms event-triggered and time-triggered subsystem refer to the paradigm employed for communication activities, i.e. whether an event message interface or a fully temporally specified state message interface is used. The communication paradigm is independent of the type of task scheduling used in the operating system, e.g., the time-triggered subsystem can use deadline scheduling to ensure timely updates of state information in the time-triggered communication controller's CNI.

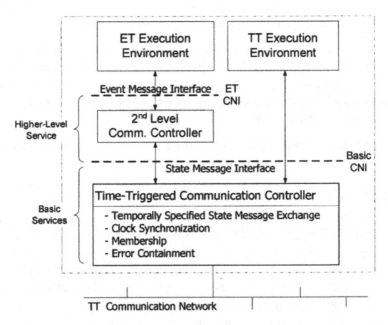

Figure 4.6.   Two Execution Environments of a Component

The component's event-triggered subsystem depends on the services of a *second level communication controller* that maps the event-triggered communication service to the underlying time-triggered transport service. The mapping occurs by layering the event-triggered messages on top of the time-triggered communication via event-triggered communication channels (ETCCs). For applications in the event-triggered subsystem, the second level communication controller offers the ability to request message disseminations at points in time determined by the applications.

Event-Triggered Task Model

A task is the execution of a sequential program. It starts with reading the input and terminates with producing the output. The time interval between the start of the task and its termination is the *execution time* of the task. This time interval depends on the inputs, the target machine, and the scheduling decisions of the operating system. In addition, the execution time depends on the progress of other tasks, if the task uses blocking synchronization statements.

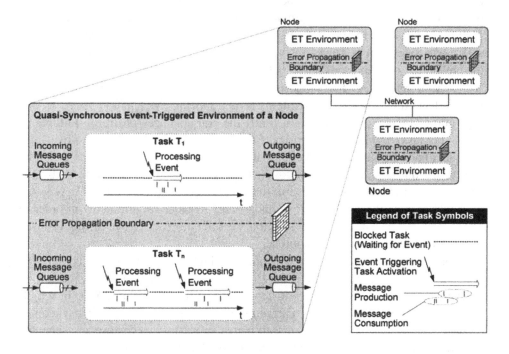

Figure 4.7. Task Model for Quasi-Synchronous Event-Triggered Subsystem

Figure 4.7 depicts the tasks running in the event-triggered quasi-synchronous subsystem of a node. The node hosts n ($n \in \mathbb{N}$) tasks T_1 to T_n. Each task T_j possesses dedicated queues, an outgoing message queue and incoming message queues. These queues are the interface between a task and the communication system.

For the event-triggered subsystem, we assume the event-based computational model in the system architecture. Initially, a task will block and wait for the occurrence of a significant event that requires a processing activity. In case such an event arrives (i.e. an event trigger), the task will be become ready and wait for being executed by the processor. During the execution of the task, it may produce messages by placing messages in its outgoing queue. Furthermore, the task can consume messages by fetching them from the task's incoming message queues. When the task finishes the processing of the event, the task will wait for the occurrence of a subsequent event.

Scheduling

The scheduler has to manage access to the CPU for tasks both in the event-triggered and time-triggered subsystems. As described in Section 3.3, the scheduler is responsible for temporal partitioning within a component. Since time-triggered tasks represent critical functions and event-triggered tasks can possess probabilistic bounds of execution times, the primary objective with respect to error containment is the prevention of temporal fault propagation from tasks in the event-triggered subsystem to tasks in the time-triggered subsystem. A secondary scheduling goal is the prevention of fault propagation between tasks in the event-triggered subsystem.

A scheduling strategy that supports error containment between tasks of the event-triggered and time-triggered subsystems is *time sharing* [McKinney, 1969]. In this scheduling strategy, a quota system limits the consequences of timing failures of tasks. For tasks implementing critical functions in the time-triggered subsystem, the quota must be sufficiently large to allow the task to finish within its deadline. Hence, the quota of a task in the time-triggered subsystem is determined by the task's worst-case execution time. For the event-triggered subsystem, it is possible to choose a quota that is biased towards average resource requirements in order to establish a more resource efficient solution, i.e. tolerating occasional timing failures in favor of a more economical approach.

Another approach is *two-level scheduling,* which uses different schedulers for tasks in the event-triggered and time-triggered subsystems. This approach is a special case of hierarchical (or multi-level) scheduling [Regehr, 2001], in which a generalized scheduler allocates CPU time to other schedulers. A first scheduler allocates CPU time to tasks in the time-triggered subsystem. It can use any scheduling strategy ensuring that tasks in the time-triggered subsystem meet their deadlines (e.g., EDF scheduling). Whenever no task in the time-triggered subsystem requests execution, control is handed over to a second scheduler, which is responsible for managing the tasks in the event-triggered subsystem. On its part, the second scheduler can use a time sharing approach to ensure error containment between different tasks in the event-triggered subsystem.

The main strength of using two-level scheduling in the proposed system architecture is the ability to decompose the scheduler into two smaller and simpler schedulers. The partly contradicting requirements of the event-triggered and time-triggered subsystems would increase the complexity of a single monolithic scheduler. For the scheduling of the time-triggered subsystem the meeting of deadlines is of paramount importance, because of the dynamics of the controlled object and the temporal obligations at the time-triggered CNI (input and output firewall). The time-triggered subsystem will, however, provide a higher level of a priori knowledge, e.g., deterministic worst-case execution times. Scheduling of the event-triggered subsystem, on the other hand, requires a higher degree of flexibility and must handle probabilistic worst-case task execution times.

Linux real-time extensions [Beal et al., 2000; Barabanov and Yodaiken, 1996] are examples of schedulers that implement such a two-level scheduling approach. A hard real-time scheduler passes control to a second scheduler, the standard Linux scheduler, whenever no hard real-time tasks request execution.

4.4 Dependability Mechanisms

This section specifies the fault hypotheses of the event-triggered and time-triggered subsystems by defining FCRs, failure mode assumptions, and failure rate assumptions. Furthermore, we describes the error containment mechanisms of the integrated system architecture.

Fault Hypothesis of the Time-Triggered Subsystems

For the time-triggered subsystems, we employ the fault hypothesis established in [Bauer et al., 2001] for the Time-Triggered Architecture. This fault hypothesis regards system components (node computers) and communication channels as FCRs. No assumption regarding the failure modes of nodes are being made. Nodes may exhibit critical failure modes as identified in [Kopetz, 2003], such as crash/omission, babbling idiot, masquerading, and slightly-off-specification (SOS) failures. The fault hypothesis claims that only one component becomes faulty every TDMA round. Further, a new node may become faulty only after the previously faulty node (if any) either has shut down or operates correctly again.

Fault Hypothesis of the Event-Triggered Subsystems

Since the event-triggered and time-triggered subsystems share the same underlying hardware, the event-triggered subsystem is also prone to hardware faults hitting common resources within a component. Consequently, the fault hypothesis of the event-triggered subsystem must also include the failure modes introduced for the time-triggered subsystem.

Additional failure modes of the event-triggered subsystem result from the quasi-synchronism and the triggering of computational and communication activities via events from the environment. These additional failure modes are timing failures, which represent violations of the message interarrival time specification of a sender, or violations of the message service time specification of a receiver. We will denote these failures as *performance failures*. An example for such a performance failure is a faulty sender that overloads its receivers, potentially resulting in buffer overflows and message losses (message omissions).

The faults leading to the additional failure modes of the quasi-synchronous event-triggered subsystem are developmental software faults (design faults) and operational software faults (interaction faults) [Avizienis et al., 2001]. Within these fault classes, the following faults are characteristic to the quasi-synchronous event-triggered subsystem:

- **Imprecise probabilistic processor models.** The construction of adequate models for execution time predictions in modern processors is complicated by micro-architecture features, such as caching, pipelining, and branch prediction [Chandra and Harmon, 1995; Engblom, 2003]. This temporal unpredictability of tasks complicates the determination of probability distributions of message interarrival and service times.

- **Imprecise probabilistic model of environment.** For events triggering computational and communication activities, knowledge about event interarrival times and correlation between events is essential for reasoning about the temporal behavior of the event-triggered subsystem. As the environment exerts temporal control, temporal uncertainty of the environment leads to temporal unpredictability of the event-triggered subsystem.

- **Occasional timing failures due to resource conflicts.** The provision of resources according to average demands is likely to cause timing failures during worst-case load scenarios. For applications in the quasi-synchronous subsystem, occasional timing failures are accepted at design time, if the probability for failures is sufficiently low (as indicated by the system feasibility probability [Hu et al., 2001]).

- **Interaction faults.** The environment interacting with the computer system provides inputs, which do not meet the input specification, based on which the computer system has been designed. For example, the frequency of inputs overloads the computer system.

Due to the probabilistic timing assumptions of the quasi-synchronous event-triggered subsystem, we assume that these design faults and interaction faults are the prevalent faults of the event-triggered subsystem. For these faults a task forms the delimiter of the immediate impact of a fault (in contrast to hardware faults hitting common resources of a component). Consequently, we distinguish *two types of FCRs* in the event-triggered subsystem. We regard components as FCRs for hardware faults, while individual tasks are FCRs for software faults. Since a component will in general host more than one task, we thereby establish a finer granularity with respect to FCRs for software faults (compared to the FCRs of the time-triggered subsystem).

Error Containment

We distinguish between error containment mechanisms for the event-triggered and time-triggered subsystems. The time-triggered subsystem prevents error propagation through message timing failures. The error containment mechanisms of the event-triggered subsystem build on top of the error containment mechanisms of the time-triggered system. At the inter-component level, the architecture handles timing and masquerading failures of event messages. At the inner-component level, the architecture prevents error propagation from the event-triggered subsystem to the time-triggered subsystem, as well as interference between different application tasks in a component's event-triggered subsystem.

Error Containment for Time-Triggered Subsystem

Error containment for the time-triggered subsystem prevents that an error that is caused by a fault in the sending FCR can propagate to another FCR via a message failure [Kopetz, 2003]. The corresponding error detection mechanisms must be in different FCRs than the message sender. Otherwise, the error detection mechanism may be impacted by the same fault that caused the message failure.

A message failure can be a message value failure or a message timing failure. Since a time-triggered system performs all communication activities at predefined points in time, the a priori knowledge about the points in time of message receptions and message transmissions can be employed for the detection of message timing failures.

An effective approach for the handling of message value failures is N-modular redundancy (NMR). For example, detection and correction of a single consistent value failure can be performed by triple modular redundancy (TMR). A prerequisite for fault-masking by voting is a consistent notion of state in the distributed FCRs, e.g., via a sparse global time base [Kopetz, 1992].

Inner-Component Error Containment for Event-Triggered Subsystem

As described in the fault hypothesis for the event-triggered subsystem, we consider event-triggered tasks as separate FCRs for software faults. In addition, we regard the software platform, which is the combination of the operating system and the component's middleware, as a FCR. The software platform operates correctly regardless of any software fault in an event-triggered application task.

The software platform performs error detection and fault isolation for application tasks. Since the software platform is replicated in all components, it represents a single point of failure for developmental software faults. Thus, the establishment of correctness for the software platform is of utmost importance. Ideally, the software platform should be formally verified.

An inner-component error containment region of the event-triggered subsystem consists of two FCRs, which are independent with respect to software faults (developmental or interaction faults [Avizienis et al., 2001]). Figure 4.8 depicts an inner-component error containment region. One FCR is an event-triggered application task, the second FCR is the software platform (operating system and middleware services) concerned with error detection. After the software platform has determined an error in the application task, the task can be isolated to avoid er-

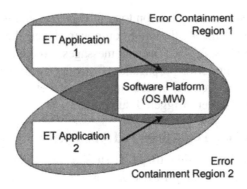

Figure 4.8. Fault-Containment Regions (Boxes) and Inner-Component Error-Containment Regions (Ellipses)

ror propagation. The software platform is responsible for spatial partitioning and temporal partitioning:

- **Temporal Partitioning by Operating System:** The operating system's scheduling strategy prevents propagation of temporal failures (see Section 3.3), both between different tasks in the event-triggered subsystem and between the event-triggered and the time-triggered subsystems.

- **Spatial Partitioning by Operating System:** The operating system controls memory protection mechanisms, e.g., via page table entries of a hardware memory management unit.

- **Temporal Partitioning by Middleware:** A sender performance failure occurs, if a sender violates its message interarrival time specification. The middleware's queue management functions have to prevent a propagation of sender performance failures, such as a faulty sender task blocking queuing capacities of correct sender tasks. Similarly, the middleware's queue management functions have to prevent a propagation of receiver performance failures. A receiver performance failure occurs, if a receiver violates its service time specification.

- **Spatial Partitioning by Middleware:** The middleware services ensure that a task can neither manipulate messages of correct tasks, nor consume messages destined for other tasks.

Inter-Component Error Containment for Event-Triggered Subsystem

At the inter-component level, the event-triggered middleware services of the software platform must ensure temporal and spatial partitioning to prevent error propagation via event message failures. As ETCCs represent elementary interfaces, error containment is only concerned with preventing error propagation from the receiver to the sender. As depicted in Figure 4.9, the application task producing

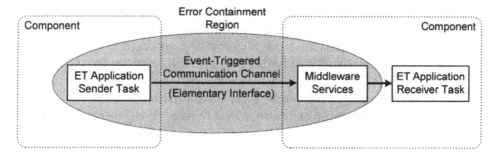

Figure 4.9. Fault-Containment Regions (Boxes) and Inter-Component Error-Containment Regions (Ellipses)

event messages and the event-triggered middleware at the receiver form an error containment region (ECR). The event-triggered middleware is part of a separate FCR, which is located in a different component. Consequently, the middleware is independent with respect to both software faults and hardware faults defined in the fault hypothesis. The middleware detects and isolates performance failures and masquerading failures. In the event-triggered subsystem, masquerading failures are a subclass of message value failures, namely event messages with invalid address information. The handling of general value failures is in the responsibility of the application. For the handling of message timing failures, the event-triggered communication system provides the following two mechanisms:

- **Separation of resources at the communication channel:** The underlying time-triggered transport protocol assigns dedicated sending slots to every ETCC. As a consequence, it separates the communication activities of different tasks. Since a task's communication activities are constrained to its ETCC, a task exhibiting a performance failure cannot block access to the communication channel for other tasks.

- **Separation of queuing resources at the node computer:** In the event-triggered service model, we provide separate incoming message queues for different ETCCs, i.e. separate queues for different sender tasks. Hence, a single faulty sender cannot affect a receiver's ability to receive event messages from correct senders. In case of a single event message queue for all ETCCs, a single sender suffering a performance failure could cause a congestion of the incoming message queue. A single faulty sender would have the potential of causing insufficient queue space for messages of correct tasks.

4.5 Membership Information

This section describes a solution to the membership problem [Cristian, 1991b] for the event-triggered subsystem. The event-triggered membership service establishes agreement on the identity of correctly functioning application tasks in the event-triggered subsystem. We start by specifying the detected failures modes (crash, omission, performance failures) and discuss the benefits of membership information for the event-triggered subsystem. Subsequently, we describe the construction of event-triggered membership information, which is based on the membership of the underlying time-triggered system. Additional local failure detectors in the synchronous time-triggered subsystem observe the behavior of the event-triggered subsystem for detecting crash and performance failures. Local membership views are exchanged via the time-triggered transport service. Since the time-triggered transport service provides an atomic broadcast, the global consistent event-triggered membership is deterministically established by applying a convergence function.

Benefits of Event-Triggered Membership Service

The event-triggered membership service detects *crash, omission,* and *performance failures.* Crash and performance failures are two classes of timing failures of event-triggered application tasks, the detection of which is performed by crash and performance failure detectors at task level.

An omission failure is a component failure (node computer or communication channel) and involves a failure of the component's time-triggered subsystem. We assume that consistent omission failures are the only failure mode of a component's time-triggered subsystem as experienced by correct components. Consequently, all message timing failures of the time-triggered system (as specified in the fault hypothesis) must be converted into consistent omission failures by the architecture. The detection of omission failures occurs through the time-triggered membership service. Since the time-triggered system regards components as FCRs, detection of omission failures occurs at component level granularity.

The detection of crash, performance, and omission failures through the event-triggered membership service provides the following benefits:

- **Systematic Error Detection:** Error detection is performed by the event-triggered communication service, i.e. depending on the implementation of the event-triggered communication service either via event-triggered middleware or a communication controller with support for ETCCs. The systematic error detection reduces complexity, since the detection of crash, omission, and performance failures need not be performed by application tasks. Application tasks can react to detected component failures as indicated through the event-triggered membership service.

- **Diagnostic Purposes:** The event-triggered membership service detects components that do not comply to agreed message production/consumption rates. The event-triggered membership service helps in collecting diagnostic information, e.g., as required by a maintenance engineer.

- **Implicit Acknowledgment of Messages and Flow Control:** As explained in Section 4.2 an ETCC uses a unidirectional control flow and represents an elementary interface. As a consequence, buffer overflows result in message omissions and can affect state synchronization. The membership service of the event-triggered subsystem allows a reaction to such message omissions, e.g., the sender can retransmit the message by becoming aware of the omission.

Basic Idea of Membership Service

As depicted in Figure 4.10, application tasks in the event-triggered subsystem send and receive messages, thereby producing a behavior observable at the time-triggered subsystem. We define *behavior* as the *temporal sequence of send and receive operations* of the event-triggered application tasks. Our definition of behavior is an extension of the definition contained in [Jones et al., 2002], which regards a system's behavior as the temporal sequence of send operations of a system. Since message receptions occur according to the information pull principle, we include message receptions in the behavior of tasks.

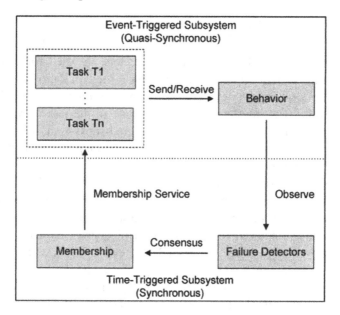

Figure 4.10. Event-Triggered Membership Construction via an Underlying Time-Triggered System

The behavior of the application tasks is observed by failure detectors in the time-triggered subsystem. Every event-triggered application task is assigned dedicated local failure detectors, which yield a local membership vector that represent the task's view regarding the operational state of itself and all other event-triggered application task. These failure detectors perform failure detection for two failure modes of event-triggered tasks, namely crash and performance failures. In addition, the time-triggered subsystem detects omission failures via the time-triggered membership service.

The local membership vectors are periodically exchanged via the time-triggered transport service. Since the time-triggered transport service offers an atomic broadcast mechanism, all components gain a consistent set of local membership views of correct components. The exchange of local views solves the interactive consistency problem, i.e. it provides a consensus vector with the local membership views.

During the next step, we map the consensus vector to a consensus value by agreeing on a single global consistent membership vector. As every component possesses the same set of local membership vectors, this agreement occurs deterministically by applying a convergence function. The resulting global consistent membership vector is provided to the event-triggered subsystem via the event-triggered membership service.

The periodic process of exchanging local membership views, agreeing on a consistent view, and updating the global consistent membership vector is called a *membership round.*

Local Failure Detectors

The middleware in the time-triggered subsystem provides dedicated local failure detectors for every task. The local failure detectors are used for constructing a local membership vector, which denotes the task's view of the operational state of other tasks. The local failure detectors operate on the *interface state* [Jones et al., 2002] of the task. The interface state is the state of the task as viewed from a particular interface. For a task in the event-triggered subsystem, the interface state at a particular point in time is the set of incoming and outgoing messages enqueued in the task's event message queues at that time.

At the service providing linking interface (SPLIF), the local failure detectors employ *output assertions,* i.e. expressions which, if evaluated to false indicate an error of the interface state. In general, an output assertion can be an arbitrary expression yielding a boolean result. A powerful approach for the specification of assertions are temporal logic variants [Bellini et al., 2000], as they support the expressing of temporal constraints. An example for a simple output assertion is a test for determining, whether an outgoing message queue is already full, when a new message arrives from the corresponding sender task. The firing of this output assertion indicates an immanent message loss due to insufficient queuing capacity.

Similarly, the local failure detectors at the service requesting linking interface (SRLIF) employ *input assertions* for error detection at incoming message queues. An examples for a simple input assertions is a test for determining, whether the incoming message queue is already full when a new message arrives from the network.

The output and input assertions used in the construction of failure detectors should incorporate the a priori knowledge about the task's behavior. Knowledge

about deterministic lower/upper bounds for the durations between message trans-
missions/receptions allows the construction of perfect failure detectors as defined
by Chandra and Toueg in [Chandra and Toueg, 1996]. Perfect failure detectors
satisfy both the *accuracy* and *completeness* requirement (see Section 2.3). A vi-
olation of accuracy leads to classifying a correct task as faulty. Completeness is
violated, if a failure remains undetected. In case of probabilistic temporal specifications, we can only *provide probabilistic failure detectors*. A probabilistic failure
detector possesses a certain probability for violating the accuracy and completeness
properties.

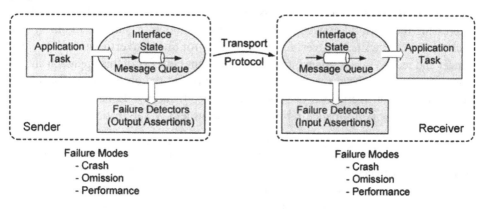

Figure 4.11. Local Failure Detectors

Figure 4.11 depicts a sender and a receiver with the corresponding failure detectors at the event-triggered SPLIF and SRLIF. Following the distinction of the three
failure modes included in the event-triggered membership service, we distinguish
three types of failure detectors: omission, performance, and crash failure detectors.

Omission Failure Detectors

All failure modes that include the underlying time-triggered subsystem of a component are mapped to message omission failures. Omission failures are detected by
the time-triggered membership service. All event-triggered tasks hosted by a component are considered as incorrect, when the time-triggered membership service
classifies the component as incorrect.

Performance Failure Detectors

We distinguish between sender and receiver performance failure detectors.
Sender performance failure detectors use the observed points in time of message
transmissions for detecting violations of a task's message interarrival time specification. *Receiver performance failure detectors* use the observed points in time
of message receptions for detecting violations of a task's message service time
specification.

The level of *accuracy* and *completeness* [Chandra and Toueg, 1996] of these performance failure detectors depends on the rigidity of the temporal specification of event-triggered tasks. Probabilistic service and interarrival time specifications will lead to *probabilistic failure detectors,* which possesses a certain probability for violating the accuracy and completeness properties of a perfect failure detector. Deterministic service and interarrival times, such as upper bounds for the time between message receptions and lower bounds for the time between message transmissions, permit the construction of perfect performance failure detectors.

In general, the construction of performance failure detectors can employ an arbitrary specification method (e.g., assertions in temporal logic) that is capable of expressing the a priori knowledge about the task's temporal behavior. In our system architecture, we will, however, focus on testing for queue overflows to determine sender and receiver performance failures. The main benefits of this approach are the lower run-time overhead for evaluating assertions and the ability to perform error detection without interarrival or service time specifications. Hence, this approach is also suited for performance failure detection in legacy applications.

Consequently, an overflow of an outgoing message queue indicates a sender performance failure. An incoming queue overflow indicates either a sender or a receiver performance failure. Following the self-confidence principle, a receiver will initially assume a sender performance failure (as denoted in its local membership view). The subsequent agreement on the global consistent membership vector clarifies whether the detected performance failure has actually been a receiver or a sender performance failure.

Crash Failure Detectors

We consider message receptions and transmissions as life signs of the corresponding event-triggered application task. The level of a priori knowledge about the behavior of an event-triggered task determines the ability for detecting crash failures through the absence of message receptions and transmissions.

In analogy to performance failure detectors, we can construct perfect crash failure detectors, if lower bounds for interarrival or service times are available. A perfect crash failure detector can also be built with knowledge about upper bounds for task execution times. In case of probabilistic knowledge about the interarrival, service, and execution times, we can only construct probabilistic crash failure detectors.

If the distribution functions for task execution times, message interarrival times, and message service times have an asymptotic behavior, the detection of crash failures has to decide on a threshold for detecting crash failures. When a task does not exhibit communication activities for an interval of time exceeding the threshold value, it is considered to have crashed. The threshold value will determine the detection latency and the probability of false crash failure detections, i.e. the threshold value limits the failure detector's accuracy. Adversely, the threshold value can be calculated based on the required probability for the accuracy of the crash failure detection.

While the probabilistic knowledge about execution times leads to probabilistic accuracy, we can always ensure completeness, because a crashed task will not continue to send or transmit messages until it is explicitly restarted.

Consistency of Distributed Failure Detections

If a task failure is part of the failure mode and rate assumptions of the membership service, the failure will lead to corresponding failure detections. Depending on the failure mode, the detections will occur locally at the failure detector associated with the faulty task (in the same component) or remotely at failure detectors associated with other tasks.

The first case, namely a *local failure detection,* applies to sender performance failures that are detected via outgoing queue overflows, as well as to crash failures that are limited to a single task (i.e. due to software faults). Since the message transmissions and (pulling) receptions represent life signs of a task, they are employed for locally detecting the task's crash failure within the component. Consequently, crash failure detection for individual tasks can only occur locally, because other components do not possess knowledge about the points in time, when a task has pulled messages out of its incoming message queues.

Remote failure detections occur for omission failures, receiver performance failures, and those sender performance that are detected through incoming message queue overflows. In general, remote failure detections occur at more than a single FCR. For example, a sender performance failure can result in failure detections through incoming queue overflows at all task's receiving the messages from the faulty sender. In order to be able to agree on a global consistent membership view, it is essential to establish a mapping between a set of remote failure detections and the corresponding failure. The establishment of this mapping is complicated, if detections of the failure at different FCRs are scattered over an interval of time.

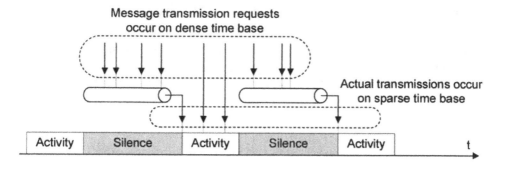

Figure 4.12. Mapping Event Message Transmissions to a Sparse Time Base

A fundamental requirement for the ability to unambiguously establish the mapping between failures and remote detections is the knowledge about a minimum interarrival time between failures, as specified in the fault hypothesis of the integrated system architecture.

The actual mapping between failures and remote detections occurs as part of the agreement on a global consistent membership vector out of local membership views. We can distinguish two approaches:

- **Error Detections on Sparse Time Base:** Although event-triggered applications are not required to send or fetch messages within the action lattice of a sparse time base [Kopetz, 1992], the communication system can restrict transmissions to predefined activity intervals, i.e. by delaying message transmissions requested during an interval of silence (see Figure 4.12).

  If the silence interval of this sparse time base has a sufficient length to compensate for the detection jitter of different failure detectors, it is guaranteed that failure detectors detect a failure within the same activity interval. Consequently, these distributed detections of a failure will be represented in the local membership views of a single interval of silence, during which all local membership views are frozen.

  A sparse time base for omission failure detections can easily be established due to the small detection jitter of omission failures, which is determined by the precision of the global time in the underlying time-triggered system.

  For performance failures, however, the detection jitter depends on the queuing capacities and the variability of interarrival and service times. In case of a large detection jitter for performance failures, it can be undesirable to delay message transmissions requested during the silence interval.

- **Error Detections on Dense Time Base:** This approach is necessary, if the detection jitter for performance failures prohibits the delaying of message transmission, as required for detections on a sparse time base. In this case, the remote detections of a single performance failure can be scattered over local membership views of multiple, successive membership rounds.

  Error detections on a dense time base have the advantage of involving no message delays related to detection jitter. On the other hand, the agreement on a global consistent membership view must consider a history of local membership views to allow majority based decisions.

Chapter 5

CONTROLLER AREA NETWORK EMULATION IN THE TIME-TRIGGERED ARCHITECTURE

The Controller Area Network (CAN) protocol [Bosch, 1991] was originally developed for in-car use. Industrial control systems and embedded networks became additional application fields [Lawrenz, 1995]. Impressive sales figures demonstrate the industrial relevance of CAN with more than 200 millions of CAN controllers sold in 2001. CAN represents an event-triggered communication protocol, i.e. the temporal control signals are derived primarily from non-time events. Among its advantages are flexibility and the ability to achieve a high average performance through the statistical multiplexing of bandwidth between components participating in the communication. However, CAN lacks essential properties for systems that have substantial timeliness and dependability requirements. The CAN protocol [Bosch, 1991] does not support fault-tolerance by network redundancy and multiple bit-flips can result in inconsistent message disseminations [Kaiser and Livani, 1999] (i.e. no atomic broadcast mechanism). Furthermore, the mechanisms for achieving a faulty node's self-deactivation may cause substantial periods of inaccessibility (2.5 ms at 1 Mbps [Verissimo et al., 1997]).

Solutions for addressing fault-tolerance by active redundancy [Rufino, 1997] and supporting a consistent atomic broadcast mechanism have been developed [Rufino et al., 1998; Kaiser and Livani, 1999; Livani, 1999], but these approaches either extend the CAN protocol or introduce a solution at the application level, thereby increasing application complexity.

In domains that have traditionally been handled by CAN, the applications of electronics currently extend to safety-critical functions, such as X-by-wire systems in the automotive area. In these safety-critical applications, a deterministic behavior with bounded transmission latencies and jitter for all safety-related messages must be guaranteed even at peak-load. Time-triggered communication protocols can provide this deterministic behavior. In addition to hard real-time performance, they support temporal composability and dependability. As a consequence time-triggered protocols are becoming more and more accepted as the communication infrastructure for safety-critical applications [Bretz, 2001; Rushby, 2001a].

Nevertheless, due to lower cost and higher flexibility, CAN is likely to continue to function as the communication service for non-critical functions (e.g., comfort electronics in a car) and safety-related functions with mechanical backup. Furthermore, existing CAN solutions constitute high financial investments and their functionality should be retained without the need of a complete redevelopment. The migration of these CAN-based applications to a time-triggered environment is therefore of major concern. Existing event-triggered CAN applications become legacy systems, i.e. information systems that resist evolution [Brodie and Stonebreaker, 1995].

Consequently, there is the need for an integrated architecture that supports both safety-critical time-triggered applications and non-critical CAN-based applications. The coexistence of a time-triggered subsystem with an event-triggered CAN subsystem offers the foundation for mixed-criticality and CAN legacy integration. This chapter presents a solution for such an integrated architecture, which establishes a CAN subsystem on top of the Time-Triggered Architecture (TTA) [Kopetz and Bauer, 2003]. The CAN communication service is a virtual overlay network on top of the time-triggered communication service, which is an instantiation of the model for the integration of event-triggered and time-triggered services presented in Chapter 4. Since the CAN communication service in the TTA imitates a physical CAN communication system, we will denote the CAN communication services in the TTA as *CAN emulation*.

This chapter starts with an overview of the TTA and CAN. In particular, we analyze properties of a conventional CAN network that are relevant for supporting the integration of CAN legacy applications without redevelopment efforts. In the second part of this chapter, we describe the construction of the CAN emulation. A second level communication controller, as introduced in Chapter 4, is responsible for relaying event-triggered CAN traffic into time-triggered communication. Therefore, we refer to the second level communication controller as *emulated CAN controller*. In order to support the integration of CAN legacy applications without redevelopment efforts, the emulated CAN controller provides the programming interface of commercial CAN controllers and establishes significant properties of a conventional CAN network.

In addition, the integration of CAN into the TTA leads to an improved CAN communication service. CAN applications benefit from the properties of the underlying reliable time-triggered architecture. Fault-tolerance mechanisms (error containment, media redundancy) are performed at the protocol level and do not increase application complexity. The absence of bit arbitration in the CAN emulation allows to provide bandwidths of more than 1 Mbps, thereby exceeding the physical limitations of a conventional CAN network.

5.1   The Time-Triggered Architecture

The Time-Triggered Architecture (TTA) provides a computing infrastructure for the design and implementation of dependable distributed real-time systems [Kopetz and Bauer, 2003]. The TTA provides the four basic services of an integrated architecture, namely a predictable fault-tolerant time-triggered transport service, clock synchronization, error containment, and a membership service. The fault-tolerant global time base, which is provided at every node, is exploited to precisely specify the linking interfaces. The underlying computational model is the time-triggered model of computation (see Section 2.5).

System Structure

The basic building block of the TTA is a node computer, which is a self-contained composite hardware/software subsystem [Kopetz and Suri, 2003]. A cluster is a set of nodes that are interconnected by two redundant communication channels. For the interconnection of nodes, the TTA distinguishes between two physical interconnection topologies, namely a TTA-bus and a TTA-star. A TTA-bus consists of replicated passive buses. Every node is connected to two independent guardians, which use the a priori knowledge about the points in time of communication activities to prevent communication outside a node's slot. In the star topology, the interconnection of nodes occurs via two replicated central guardians. The star topology has the advantage of a higher level of independence, since guardians are located at a physical distance from nodes. Furthermore, guardians reshape signals and support additional monitoring services [Ademaj et al., 2003].

Communication Protocol TTP/C

For providing the communication service, the TTA employs the fault-tolerant protocol TTP/C [Kopetz, 1999b], which provides the following services:

- The TTP/C protocol uses TDMA to control the media access to the two independent communication channels. Time is partitioned into slots, which are statically assigned to nodes. A sequence of slots that allows each node to send a message forms a TDMA round. A sequence of predefined TDMA rounds is called a cluster cycle. The cluster cycle also defines the periodicity of the message transmissions. Information about the points in time of all message transmissions during a cluster cycle are contained in the message schedule.

- TTP/C provides fault-tolerant clock synchronization via the Fault-Tolerant Average (FTA) clock synchronization algorithm [Lundelius and Lynch, 1984]. The clock synchronization algorithm of the TTA has been formally verified in [Pfeifer et al., 1999]. It differs from other algorithms by the fact that no special synchronization messages are used for the exchange of the local clock values of nodes. The difference between the expected and the actual arrival time of an incoming message is used to estimate the deviation between the local clock of the receiver and the sender. Furthermore, TTP/C provides support to collect timing information only from selected nodes, thereby nodes with inferior oscillators can be left out as inputs for clock synchronization.

■ The membership service provides nodes with consistent information about the operational state of every node in the cluster. In case multiple cliques with different membership views form, clique avoidance ensures that the minority cliques leave the membership [Bauer and Paulitsch, 2000].

TTP/C distinguishes between two types of messages, namely initialization frames (i-frames) and normal frames (n-frames). I-frames carry the part of the controller state, which is required for the startup and the reintegration of nodes. This subset of the controller state is denoted as c-state and includes the current position in the communication schedule, the global time, and the membership vector. N-frames are used during normal operation and carry application data. Both i-frames and n-frames are protected by CRC checks. In n-frames, CRC checking is also used for enforcing agreement on the controller states. The sender calculates the CRC of an n-frame over the message contents and the c-state of the sender. At the receiver, the CRC of an n-frame is calculated over the received message contents and the c-state of the receiver. Consequently, different c-states at the receiver and the sender will produce a negative result of the CRC check and result in a message omission failure.

Design Principles of the TTA

The TTA has been guided by the following design principles [Kopetz and Bauer, 2003; Kopetz, 1997]:

■ **Consistent Distributed Computing Base:**   The TTA simplifies the design of distributed algorithms by providing a fault-tolerant atomic broadcast service and consistent membership information at the protocol level. Within the fault hypothesis, the fault-tolerant atomic broadcast service ensures that a message sent by a correct node is received by all other correct nodes. For the construction of membership information, the TTA performs error detection by exploiting the a priori knowledge about the points in time of message transmissions.

■ **System Wide Definition of Distributed State:** The sparse time base of the TTA allows the system wide definition of distributed state, which is a prerequisite for masking failures by voting.

■ **Separation of Concerns:** Organizing interfaces by domain effectively filters information and helps in managing the complexity that is inherent in the development and evolution of large systems [Ran and Xu, 1997]. The TTA distinguishes between three types of interfaces: a real-time service (RS) interface, a diagnostic and management (DM) interface, and a configuration and planning (CP) interface. The RS interface is a time-critical interface that must meet the temporal specification of the application in all specified load and fault scenarios. The TTA uses the temporal firewall interface (see Chapter 2.4) as the RS interface. The RS and DM interfaces are used for diagnosis and configuration and are usually not time-critical.

- **Composability:** An architecture is composable with respect to a specific property, if the property is not refuted by the system integration, once it has been establishment at the subsystem level [Kopetz, 1997]. The TTA has been designed for meeting composability with respect to temporal correctness by supporting four necessary conditions for temporal composability [Kopetz, 2001]: an independent development of nodes, stability of prior services, constructive integration of nodes, and replica determinism.

5.2 Controller Area Network

This section describes the CAN protocol and discusses its strengths and deficiencies.

CAN Protocol

CAN (Controller Area Network) belongs to the class of event-triggered communication protocols. It uses a broadcast bus with "Carrier Sense, Multiple Access with Collision Avoidance" (CSMA/CA) for medium access control [Bosch, 1991]. The bit transmission takes two possible representations. The recessive state appears only on the bus when all nodes send recessive bits. The dominant state occurs, if at least one node sends a dominant bit.

A given bit-stream is transmitted using the "Non-Return-to-Zero" (NRZ) code. Bit stuffing prevents that more than five consecutive bits of identical polarity are transmitted. A node delays its transmission if the busline is busy. If the bus is idle the node can start sending. Bus access conflicts are resolved by observing the message identifier bits on the bus-line. While transmitting a message identifier, each node monitors the serial bus-line. If the transmitted bit is recessive and a dominant bit is monitored, the node gives up from transmitting and starts to receive incoming data. The node sending the object with the lowest identifier will succeed and acquire bus access. The information exchange occures using four types of protocol data frames:

1 *Data frames* are used for the transmission of CAN message objects. A data frame contains a unique identifier, which identifies the message object and denotes the message priority.

2 By transmitting a *remote frame* the dissemination of a communication object is explicitly requested. For the same identifier, the data frame takes precedence over the remote transmission request.

3 An *error frame* is used for error signaling.

4 The *overload frame* serves the purpose of extending the interframe space to handle overload conditions.

After a loss in the arbitration process or the reception of an error frame, the sender automatically performs a retransmission of the corresponding communication object. The integrity of data and remote frames is checked through a 15-bit cyclic redundancy code (CRC). The CRC checking is only performed on data and remote frames. The data rate of CAN depends on the maximum network length. Typical values for network length and data rate are 40 m and 1 Mbps. Usually a twisted-pair cable is used as the transmission medium.

Strengths and Deficiencies

In non safety-critical applications, the CAN protocol offers the following advantages:

- **Low Worst-Case Latency for Highest Priority Message:** The worst-case latency for the highest priority message results from its own transmission duration and the maximum transmission duration of a lower priority message. Since CAN is non-preemptive, the dissemination of the highest priority message can be delayed by a message that is currently in transit. When basic CAN frames [Bosch, 1991] are exchanged on a 1 Mbps CAN network, the worst-case latency for the highest priority message is below **200 μs**.

- **High Average Performance:** The dynamic multiplexing of bandwidth among nodes increases average performance. If occasional timing failures are acceptable, dynamic multiplexing also allows for more cost-effective solutions by taking the average message load generated by nodes as the basis for the dimensioning of network resources.

- **Flexibility and Strong Migration Support:** A CAN system allows the migration of an application function F to a different node without requiring any modifications at other nodes. The migration occurs transparently to functions that interact with F. This transparency is also a prerequisite for the transfer of functions while the system is running, which is referred to as *strong migration* [Ghezzi and Vigna, 1997].

- **Low Hardware Cost:** The widespread use of CAN has resulted in high volume productions of numerous stand-alone CAN controllers and processors with integrated CAN support. An overview of CAN controller chips that are available on the market can be found in [CAN in Automation, 2003].

The CAN protocol possesses the following properties, which are undesirable in distributed real-time systems:

- **Variability in Transmission Latencies:** A CAN communication system possesses a large variability in the transmission latencies, because the transmission latency of a message depends on the network load. In addition, the handling of communication failures with retransmissions (timing redundancy) results in increased communication latencies in the presence of faults.

Work on the timing analysis of a CAN network in the presence of faults has been performed in [Tindell and Burns, 1994; Punnekkat et al., 2000]. These papers mainly differ in the fault assumptions. For example, in [Tindell and Burns, 1994] a worst-case number of consecutive erroneous frames is taken as the basis for the calculation of the effects of faults on the transmission latency of a message. In [Punnekkat et al., 2000], on the other hand, multiple sources of interference are assumed with each source inducing an undefined bus value during a characteristic period of time.

- **Inaccessibility Times:** Handling of node failures is performed with error counters by recording receive and transmit errors. A threshold is defined for entering the error passive mode. In this mode, a node must wait for a minimum idle time on the bus before starting a transmission. If bus contention is low, this strategy results in the interleaving of correct and invalid messages. If a node's error counter exceeds a second threshold, the node enters the bus-off state.

  Under the assumption that failed nodes reach the bus-off state, the worst-case inaccessibility time at 1 Mbps is bounded by 2.5ms [Verissimo et al., 1991; Rufino and Verissimo, 1995].

- **Limited Throughput:** The arbitration logic of CAN limits throughput, because the propagation delay of the channel must be smaller than the length of a bit cell. A CAN network of 40 m results in a maximum bandwidth of 1 Mbps.

Furthermore, the CAN protocol does not address the following problems:

- **Membership Problem:** No membership service is provided at the protocol level.

- **Clock Synchronization:** The CAN protocol does not include a clock synchronization service. If a global notion of time is required, it must be implemented at the application level.

- **Babbling Idiot Failure Handling:** CAN does not prevent babbling idiot failures [Kopetz, 1997]. A node can continuously send highest priority messages and thereby prevent communication of other nodes.

- **Temporal Composability:** The temporal properties of a CAN system are changed during the integration of the system. The transmission of a message is triggered explicitly by a transmission request from the application. The temporal coordination of the communication activities is a global issue and depends on the application software in all nodes.

- **Fault-Tolerant Atomic Broadcast:** CAN error recovery mechanisms are unable to ensure a consistent state, if an error is detected in the last but one bit of a frame. Possible consequences are an inconsistent message duplication or an inconsistent message ordering. Establishing consistency requires modifications to the host software [Rufino et al., 1998; Kaiser and Livani, 1999] or a dedicated hardware component [Livani, 1999].

Latencies of a CAN Network

According to [Tindell and Burns, 1994] a bound for the maximum transmission latency of a CAN message m is:

$$R_m = J_m + w_m + C_m, \tag{5.1}$$

where J_m is the queuing jitter of the message m, which depends on task response times. w_m denotes the worst-case queuing delay due to higher priority messages and lower priority messages that already obtained the bus. C_m is the longest time required to physically send the messages on the CAN network. C_m depends on the bit time on the bus τ_{bit}, the message size s_m in bytes, and the message format.

$$C_m = \left(\left\lfloor \frac{(b_{control} - 13) + 8 \cdot s_m}{5} \right\rfloor + b_{control} + 8 s_m \right) \cdot \tau_{bit}, \tag{5.2}$$

with $b_{control} = 47$ for standard CAN frames, and $b_{control} = 67$ for extended CAN frames. The worst-case queuing delay has been identified in [Tindell and Burns, 1994] as

$$w_m = B_m + \sum_{\forall j \in hp(m)} \left\lceil \frac{w_m + J_j + \tau_{bit}}{T_j} \right\rceil \cdot C_j, \tag{5.3}$$

where $hp(m)$ denotes the set of messages with higher priority than m. T_j denotes the period of message m. B_m is the longest time message m can be delayed by lower priority messages. Hence, B_m is the maximum time to physically send a message out of the set of messages $lp(m)$ with lower priority than m.

$$B_m = \max_{\forall k \in lp(m)} \{C_k\} \tag{5.4}$$

For the highest priority message h the set $hp(h)$ of higher priority is empty. Hence w_h is equal to B_h and the maximum transmission latency for message h is as follows:

$$R_h = J_h + \max_{\forall k \in lp(h)} \{C_k\} + C_h \tag{5.5}$$

In the presence of faults, the calculation of R_h must take into account the possibility of inaccessibility times [Verissimo and Marques, 1990] of the CAN communication service.

5.3 Requirements and Objectives

This section describes the objectives and requirements for the integration of CAN communication services into a time-triggered architecture. In particular, we address the requirements for the reuse of CAN-based legacy applications. The establishment of the programming interface of commercial CAN controllers, as well as the reproduction of the temporal behavior of a conventional CAN network are prerequisites for the reuse of CAN-based legacy applications without redevelopment and retesting efforts.

Objectives of CAN Emulation

The provision of CAN communication services in a time-triggered architecture serves the following purposes:

- **Reuse of CAN-based Legacy Applications:** In case the introduction of safety-critical functions into an existing system (e.g., X-by-wire functions in automotive electronic systems) enforces a shift to the time-triggered control paradigm, a CAN communication service within a time-triggered architecture permits a gradual evolution of the system through reusing legacy application software.

- **Mixed-Criticality Systems:** High average performance and flexibility make the CAN communication service well-suited for sporadic, non time-critical communication activities (e.g., control of body electronics in a car).

- **Integration of Diverse Networks:** An important goal of the CAN integration is the interconnection of emulated and physical CAN networks. Gateways between the CAN emulation and physical CAN networks extend the potential for reusability from application software modules to complete legacy CAN clusters (a set of legacy components interconnected by a dedicated physical CAN network).

- **Increased Dependability:** Another goal of the integration of CAN into a time-triggered architecture is the construction of an improved CAN communication service. The fault-tolerance mechanisms of the underlying time-triggered system are to be exploited for increasing the dependability of the CAN subsystem.

- **Requirement of Additional Services:** The integration provides additional services (e.g., membership information, global time) to CAN-based applications. These services are mapped to the services of the underlying time-triggered system and do not increase application complexity.

- **Exceeding of Bandwidth Limitations:** The emulated CAN communication service does not perform bit arbitration, thus permitting bandwidths above 1 Mbps (maximum bandwidth of a conventional CAN network).

Reproduction of Significant Properties

For the integration of CAN into a time-triggered architecture, we have identified significant properties of messages transmitted via a conventional CAN network. For a given set of message transmission requests, these properties include the points in time when messages become permanent, the message ordering, the intervals of time during which pending transmission requests can be canceled, and the message transmission latencies.

Permanence of Messages

A message becomes *permanent,* if all earlier messages have arrived or will never arrive [Kopetz, 1997]. Since the processing of a message can be influenced by earlier messages, a message should not be acted upon until permanence is reached. A mechanism is required for determining when a message transmitted via the emulated CAN communication service becomes permanent. For this purpose, knowledge about the point in time at which the transmission would have started on a physical CAN bus is essential. A CAN message must not be revealed to the application before this point in time.

Message Ordering

CAN is an event-triggered communication protocol, which allows applications to explicitly request message transmissions. Depending on the message priorities and the points in time of the transmission requests, a certain succession of message transmissions will occur on a CAN bus. This succession of message transmissions results in a corresponding ordering of message receptions, as visible to an application in the CAN system.

Many existing CAN-based systems do not provide a priori knowledge about the temporal behavior of communication activities. As a consequence, these systems do not rely on a particular ordering of messages. Nevertheless, in the presence of restrictions about the temporal behavior of nodes, correctness of existing CAN-based applications can depend on a particular message ordering. In order to effectively support all CAN-based legacy applications, the CAN emulation must support the provision of an identical message ordering compared to a conventional CAN network, i.e. the CAN emulation has to reveal messages to the application in the same order as a conventional CAN communication system.

Ability to Cancel Messages

When an application passes a CAN message to its CAN controller, the corresponding message transmission is delayed until the bus becomes idle and the message wins in the arbitration process. Before this point in time, the message can still be canceled by the application at the sender. In the CAN emulation, a CAN message must not be visible to applications at receiving nodes while the message is still cancelable.

Transmission Latencies

In a CAN network, the transmission latency of a message depends on the bus state at the point in time of the transmission request and the set of higher priority messages competing for bus access. There are several levels of authenticity with respect to emulated latencies that can be established:

L1 Exact reproduction of CAN transmission latencies: This level of emulation involves support for best-case latencies of a conventional CAN communication system. Best-case latencies are determined by the bit length of messages and the network's bit rate. The best-case latency for a message is observed, if no channel failure occurs, no transmission is currently in progress, and no higher priority messages are pending.

L2 Assuring upper bounds for transmission latencies of a conventional CAN network: In a CAN communication system, the smallest guaranteed message transmission latency can be established for the highest priority message. In the worst-case, the transmission of the highest priority message is delayed by another CAN message of maximum size, which has progressed beyond the arbitration field when the sending of the message is requested.

L3 Transmission latencies of a CAN network in the presence of communication faults: If the reproduction of temporal guarantees in the presence of faults is sufficient, the duration of CAN inaccessibility times can serve as the basis for the determination of acceptable transmission latencies.

L4 Best-effort CAN services: A minimum latency is targeted with the available processing and communication resources.

The emulation level with respect to transmission latencies should be statically selectable by the user, who can thereby establish a trade-off between resources provided for the CAN subsystem and the time-triggered subsystem. The CAN emulation has to support all emulation levels except the first one, which would require the provision of CAN best-case latencies. Due to the non-preemptive nature of CAN, legacy applications cannot rely on level L1 in a conventional CAN network, either.

Application Interface Requirements

The CAN emulation supports two major types of applications. Legacy applications expect the interface of a particular CAN controller. Newly developed applications can benefit from additional services and bandwidths above 1 Mbps. By providing dedicated interfaces for these two types of applications, we can establish a separation of concerns. The *extended CAN interface* is designed for newly developed CAN-based applications and provides additional services (membership service, global time). CAN-based legacy applications access the CAN emulation through the *register interface*, which offers the register set of a commercial CAN controller. An emulation at the register level is independent of higher-level APIs (e.g., CANopen [CAN in Automation, 1996], CAN Kingdom [Fredriksson, 1995], DeviceNet [Noonen et al., 1994]) and supports CAN applications directly accessing the CAN controller's registers.

5.4   CAN Communication Services in the TTA

The CAN emulation in the TTA is an instantiation of the system architecture for the integration of event-triggered and time-triggered services as described in Chapter 4. The TTA (see Figure 5.1) is a waist-line architecture that distinguishes between formally analyzed and validated basic services and higher-level services that build on top of these basic services. The CAN emulation is an example of a higher-level service, for which the basic services provide the foundation.

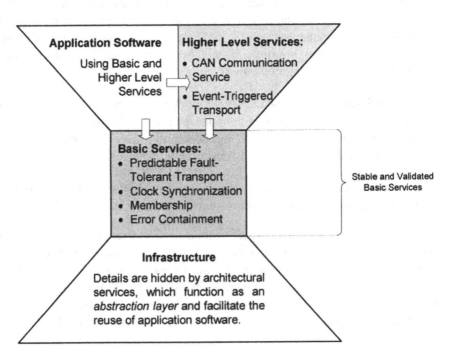

Figure 5.1. TTA Waist-Line Architecture with Higher-Level CAN Communication Service

A node, which is depicted in Figure 5.2 offers two subsystems: a time-triggered subsystem and a CAN subsystem. The time-triggered subsystem supports applications directly processing the state information contained in CNI of the time-triggered communication controller. The CAN subsystem is designed for CAN-based applications, which communicate event-triggered by requesting message disseminations at the emulated CAN controller.

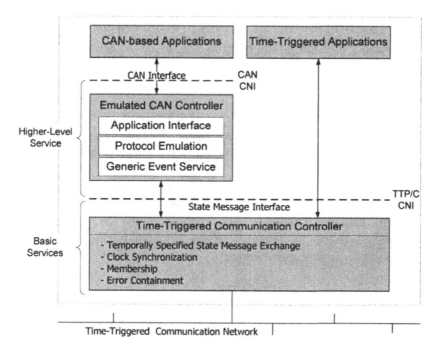

Figure 5.2. Node with Time-Triggered and CAN-based Applications

The emulated CAN controller is composed of three layers, namely a *generic event service layer,* a *protocol emulation layer,* and an *application interface layer.* These three layers perform a stepwise refinement of the TTP/C controller's state message interface into the CAN interface of a particular commercial CAN controller. Layering is a common technique to simplify the design of communication protocols by dividing them into functional layers (e.g., TCP/IP [Deering and Hinden, 1998], ISO/OSI network model [International Standardization Organisation, 1994]).

The generic event service layer performs the dissemination of event messages via the underlying time-triggered communication service. This layer establishes an event-triggered communication channel (ETCC), as introduced in Chapter 4. The sequence of transmission requests at a node results in a sequential data stream of event messages. The generic event service layer fragments this message stream into packets, which are placed into dedicated slots (CAN slots) of the underlying time-triggered communication schedule. The CAN protocol emulation layer reproduces the behavior of the conventional CAN network by performing an incremental discrete event simulation of the emulated CAN network. The application interface offers the programming interface of a specific CAN controller for CAN-based legacy applications. It also supports the queue management and message filtering functionality performed by existing CAN controllers.

The three layers of the emulated CAN controller interact only via specified interfaces, thus allowing to adapt or replace layers independently of each other. For example, the application interface can be replaced in order to emulate a different commercial CAN controller without requiring any changes to the protocol emulation or event service layer.

Generic Event Service

The generic event service layer provides a packet service for mapping a state message interface into an event message interface. This mapping is the foundation for the transport of event messages on top of the underlying time-triggered communication protocol.

A fraction of a node's slot forms its CAN slot, which is dedicated to the transmission of event messages. The rest of the slot can be used for the transmission of periodic real-time data (see Figure 5.3). The proportion of the CAN slot is application specific and determines the resource consumption, bandwidth, and latency of the event-triggered communication service.

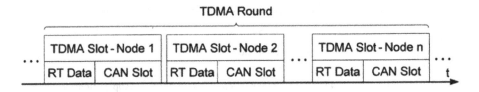

Figure 5.3. TDMA Round with Slots for Event Messages

The primary functions of the event service layer are the fragmentation of outgoing event messages into packets and the reassembly of incoming packets into event messages. The event service layer puts packets of outgoing messages into the time-triggered communication controller's CNI, thereby arranging for the dissemination of the packets through the time-triggered communication service. The time-triggered communication controller treats packets in the CNI as state information, broadcasting them on the network during the node's CAN slot. Depending on the size of the CAN slot, it is possible for packets from multiple event messages to be placed into the CAN slot. Furthermore, the time-triggered communication controller places received packets, which have been communicated via the CAN slots of other nodes, in the CNI. The event service layer retrieves these incoming packets from the CNI and fuses them into event messages.

As depicted in Figure 5.4, event message queues form the interface between the event service layer and higher protocol layers or application tasks. Every applica-

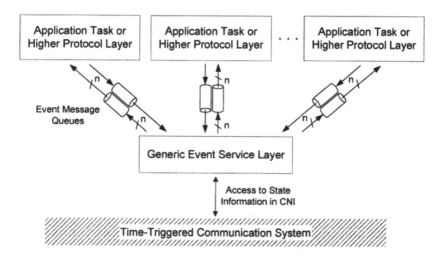

Figure 5.4. Interface Between Generic Event Service Layer and Adjacent Layers

tion or higher-level protocol task interfacing the event service layer is assigned a dedicated set of event message queues. For every task, this set consists of a single outgoing message queue and a separate incoming message queue for every ETCC the task reads from. By offering separate incoming message queues for different senders, a single faulty sender cannot affect a receiver's ability to receive event messages from correct senders.

Message Types

The CAN emulation distinguishes two types of messages. *Extended CAN messages* carry user data, while *CAN initialization-messages* are used during startup and reintegration.

Extended CAN Messages

The emulated CAN controller builds an extended CAN message by extending the CAN message generated by the application with additional control flags (request flag, identifier type, cancellation request flag) and a timestamp. The purpose of the additional attributes is the ability to transmit CAN messages on top of the time-triggered communication service, while preserving the communication semantics of a conventional CAN network. CAN messages that are transmitted over an ETCC have a size between 7 and 17 bytes (see Table 5.1). The length field specifies the size of the extended CAN message. It also indicates the beginning of the next message. The timestamp in the extended CAN message stores the point in time when the emulated CAN controller at the sending node was handed over the message for being sent. The request flag serves the purpose of triggering the transmission of the message with the specified identifier at the receiver. The identifier type flag is used

Table 5.1.   Extended CAN Message

entry	size	meaning
length field	8 bit	message length in bytes
timestamp	32 bit	transmission request timestamp
request flag	1 bit	request of message object dissemination
identifier type	1 bit	standard or extend identifier
cancellation request	1 bit	cancellation of a message object
identifier	11 or 29 bit	message priority, identifies message
datafield	0-8 bytes	0-8 bytes of data

to distinguish between standard and extended CAN messages. The cancellation request flag informs receiving nodes about the cancellation of the message with the specified identifier. The identifier denotes both a specific message object and the message priority.

CAN Initialization-Messages

CAN initialization-messages carry the subset of the state of the emulated CAN controller that is required for startup and reintegration. This subset of the state is the current position in the message fragmentation process. The event service layers at all nodes require consistent knowledge about this position for being able to reassemble messages out of packets. Since no explicit message delimiters are exchanged via an ETCC, a node requires CAN initialization-messages to gain initial synchronization in the fragmentation and assembly of messages.

The current fragmentation position in a CAN initialization-message sent by a node denotes the remainder of the currently communicated event message via the node's ETCC, enabling an unintegrated receiver to gain knowledge about the subsequent message starting point (see Figure 5.5). The delimiters of future messages can be inferred from the length fields in messages. Furthermore, a newly integrating node introduces itself to the ensemble of nodes through a CAN initialization-message, which informs other nodes about the delimiters of messages from that node.

By scheduling the execution of the event service layer in a predefined phase-shift relationship with the time-triggered exchange of CAN slot data, changes of the state variables containing the fragmentation positions can be constrained to the action lattice of a sparse time base. For the construction of CAN initialization-messages, the emulated CAN controller at each node captures the fragmentation position in a silence interval of this sparse time base. Each node transmits the CAN initialization-messages during the node's CAN slot in periodically recurring TDMA rounds called *reintegration rounds*. Receiving nodes identify received data as CAN initialization-messages by using the global time base for the detection of reintegration rounds. The delay between successive reintegration rounds determines

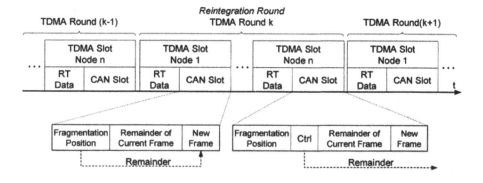

Figure 5.5. TDMA Round with Control Bytes for Node-Integration

the overhead imposed by CAN initialization-messages, as well as the reintegration and startup delays.

Protocol Emulation

The protocol emulation layer performs a discrete event simulation of a physical CAN network in order to establish significant properties of CAN (message permanence, message ordering, ability to cancel messages). This section describes an algorithm for performing this simulation. For each message, the protocol emulation algorithm determines message permanence with respect to the simulated CAN network. The algorithm provides the correct ordering for a sequence of messages and restores the ability to cancel messages by delaying received messages until reaching the point in time, when the transmission would have started on a physical CAN network. If a cancellation request is received before that time, the corresponding CAN message is discarded. Otherwise, the CAN message is revealed to the application.

The protocol emulation algorithm is fully decentralized and runs in all nodes participating in the CAN emulation. It forms the protocol emulation layer, which exchanges CAN messages with its adjacent layers, namely the application interface layer and the event service layer. A detailed description of the protocol emulation algorithm can be found in [Obermaisser, 2004b].

When the application interface passes a CAN message m to the protocol emulation, it assigns a transmission request timestamp $t_{request}$ to the message m. Let us consider the case, that the message m is not sent via the CAN emulation, but the transmission occurs on a conventional, physical CAN network. The transmission request time represented by $t_{request}$ marks the earliest point in time, when the corresponding CAN message can be transmitted on the physical CAN network. The actual start of the transmission depends on the request times and priorities of m and those messages competing with m for bus access. The transmission start of message m will be delayed, until at some future point in time the bus is idle and the priority of message m is larger than the priorities of all other pending message transmission requests.

The protocol emulation layer collects all extended CAN messages. These extended CAN messages are not yet actual CAN message transmissions, but can be seen as CAN transmission requests with prefetched message contents. They are stored in intermediate data structures of the protocol emulation layer. Based on these transmission requests, the protocol emulation simulates the behavior of a conventional CAN network. It identifies messages, which have become CAN-permanent. For a CAN-permanent message it is known, that all earlier CAN messages have been transmitted or will never be transmitted.

When a message becomes CAN-permanent, the protocol emulation layer performs a simulation step in the discrete event simulation of the physical CAN network. It updates its simulation data structures representing the state of the simulated CAN network. Thereby, it lays ground for determining CAN-permanence of subsequent CAN messages. The events triggering simulation steps are the transitions of non CAN-permanent messages to CAN-permanent messages.

Before the CAN-permanence of a message can be determined, a message must be permanent with respect to the ETCCs. We will denote this permanence as ETCC-permanence. A CAN message m is ETCC-permanent, if no message with an earlier transmission request timestamp can be received via an ETCC. For determining ETCC-permanence, we exploit the fact that transmission request timestamps of messages received via an ETCC are monotonically increasing. The monotony of the transmission request timestamps results from the fact, that for every ETCC there is only a single sender, which exclusively sends messages via the ETCC.

After the CAN-permanence of a message has been determined, the message can be revealed to the application. Due to the non-preemptive nature of CAN, knowledge of a message's CAN-permanence also involves certainty of the message being no longer cancelable. In case the protocol emulation layer receives a cancellation request before a message becomes permanent, it simply removes the messages from its intermediate data structures.

The presented algorithm also establishes the ordering relation of a conventional CAN network. The transitions of non-permanent messages to CAN-permanent messages occur in the order that would result from the messages being disseminated on a conventional CAN network.

Application Interface

The application interface layer constitutes the front-end for the CAN-based application. It emulates the programming interface of a specific CAN controller by providing the corresponding register set. Control of CAN communication services is mapped to this register set. Furthermore, the application interface layer provides the filtering and queue management services of a particular CAN controller. Acceptance filtering allows to define subsets of the message identifier space for discarding irrelevant messages and to avert buffer overruns. The filtering capabilities depend on the type of the emulated CAN controller. CAN controllers with intermediate buffers (BasicCAN chips) support limited acceptance filtering. They consider only the 8 most significant bits of the identifier. CAN controllers with object storage (FullCAN chips) support full acceptance filtering. These controllers also support scheduling strategies in case of several simultaneous transmission requests.

The CAN emulation in the TTA [Obermaisser, 2003a] supports two widely used commercial CAN controllers, namely the Intel i82527 [Intel Corporation, 1995] and the Philips SJA1000 [Philips Semiconductors, 2000].

5.5 Implementation

For the implementation of CAN communication services in the TTA, we have used a cluster of TTP monitoring nodes [TTTech, 2002a] interconnected by a redundant 25 Mbps TTP/C network.

Hardware Platform – TTP/C Monitoring Nodes

The implementation of the CAN communication service on top of TTA employs TTP monitoring nodes [TTTech, 2002a], which are equipped with the TTP-C2 controller (AS8202) and the Motorola embedded PowerPC processor MPC855T [Motorola, 2001]. The monitoring node supports synchronous (25 Mbps) and asynchronous (Modified Frequency Modulation (MFM) – 5 Mbps) bus interfaces for establishing the TTP/C communication channel. For the synchronous bus interface, it employs a 100BASE-TX physical layer with the Media Independent Interface (MII) forming the bus towards the physical interfaces.

Software Platform – Operating System RTAI Linux

The TTP monitoring node uses the embedded real-time Linux variant Real-Time Application Interface (RTAI) [Beal et al., 2000] as its operating system. RTAI combines a real-time hardware abstraction layer (RTHAL) with a real-time application interface for making Linux suitable for hard real-time applications [Mantegazza et al., 2000]. RTAI introduces a real-time scheduler, which runs the conventional Linux operating system kernel as the idle task, i.e. non real-time Linux only executes when there are no real-time tasks to run, and the real-time kernel is inactive.

In order to prevent temporal fault propagation from the Linux kernel to the real-time kernel, the real-time kernel is never blocked by the Linux side. For example, the communication links for transferring data between real-time tasks and standard Linux are non-blocking on the real-time side. Both the real-time tasks and the real-time scheduler are executed in the Linux kernel address space, which minimizes task switching times. However, a fault occurring in a real-time task can crash the system.

CAN Emulation Middleware

The implementation of the CAN emulation uses RTAI-Linux for enforcing temporal and spatial partitioning between CAN applications and time-triggered applications, as well as between different CAN applications. Time-triggered applications run in kernel space and are scheduled by the RTAI scheduler. CAN applications execute in user space and compete with standard Linux applications and the Linux kernel for resources (see Figure 5.6). The middleware services for the implementation of the CAN emulation are located both in user and kernel space. The decision on the placement of middleware tasks in user or kernel space was mainly governed by the respective necessity for direct hardware access (e.g., C2 controller). Functionality that does not require kernel space privileges has been moved to user space.

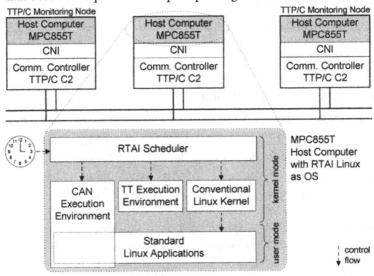

Figure 5.6. TTP/C Node with CAN and Time-Triggered Execution Environments

In kernel space, an event-triggered transport module offers the generic event service on top of TTP/C. The event service is independent of the CAN emulation and has also been employed in the establishment of different event-triggered communication protocols (e.g., transport for hard-real time CORBA broker [Segarra et al., 2003], TCP/IP [NextTTA, 2003]). The invocation of the event-triggered transport occurs via temporal control signals from the C2 TTP/C controller. The C2 controller triggers an interrupt at a priori specified global points in time. The corresponding interrupt handler is located in the event-triggered transport module, where it is invoked by the RTAI executive.

In user space, the CAN middleware task performs protocol emulation and establishes the register-level programming interface. The activation of the CAN middleware occurs periodically via a control signal from the event-triggered transport that causes the Linux kernel to schedule the middleware task.

Chapter 6

RESULTS AND VALIDATION

This chapter describes the validation results for the emulated CAN communication service of the integrated system architecture. We use analytical arguments in combination with simulation and measurements activities to demonstrate the ability of the CAN emulation to handle the communication needs of legacy and newly developed CAN applications. The implementation of the CAN emulation has been tested with message traffic from a "real-world" application provided by the automotive industry. In addition, we have applied synthetic traffic patterns in order to investigate the behavior of the event service and the CAN emulation under message loads exceeding 1 Mbps.

The protocol emulation algorithm has shown to be effective in restoring the significant properties of a conventional CAN network, which have been identified in Section 5.2. No differences in message ordering and cancelability have been observed. A comparison of transmission latencies has demonstrated similar transmission latencies in the CAN emulation and a conventional CAN network. While the CAN emulation exceeds with respect to worst-case latencies, the conventional CAN network provides superior best-case latencies.

This chapter starts with a specification of the validation objectives. It, then, analytically describes the transmission latencies of an event-triggered communication channel on top of a time-triggered communication system. The latencies of event message transmissions are related to fundamental parameters of a time-triggered communication schedule (round length, slot sizes). The second major part of this chapter focuses on the measurement and simulation activities. We first introduce the underlying message model that has been employed for defining input message sets. A MATLAB/Simulink-based simulation framework is used for determining the behavior of a conventional CAN network when provided with these message sets as inputs. The behavior of the CAN emulation is determined with a measurement framework, which contains a TTP/C cluster with the implementation of the CAN emulation. The chapter ends with a discussion of the analytical, measurement, and simulation results. Figure 6.1 contains an overview of the presented validation activities.

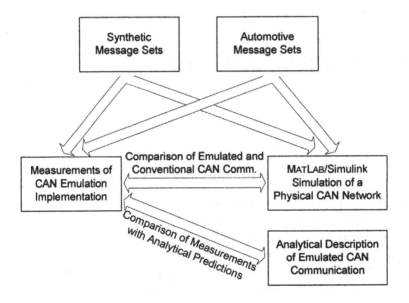

Figure 6.1. Validation Activities

6.1   Validation Objectives

The validation activities have evaluated the CAN emulation's ability to handle the communication needs of CAN-based legacy applications and newly developed CAN applications.

A primary goal of our validation activities has been the investigation, whether the emulated CAN communication service can replace physical CAN networks in the hereditary domains of CAN. As the automotive industry has been a driving force for the development of the integrated architecture with CAN communication services, we have applied message traffic from an automotive application for this evaluation.

Currently, powertrain CAN networks possess the highest bandwidth and dependability requirements of CAN networks in cars. Powertrain networks interconnect safety-related functions with mechanical backups, such as electronic stability programs. Consequently, we have used message traffic from a powertrain CAN network for the validation of the CAN communication service.

Another objective has been the demonstration of the CAN emulation being capable of exceeding the physical limitations of a conventional CAN network. As the usage of electronics is steadily increasing (e.g., the Volkswagen Phaeton contains up to 61 ECUs [Hansen Report, 2002], the BMW 7 contains up to 75 ECUs [Deicke, 2002]), it can be expected that the maximum bandwidth of 1 Mbps of a conventional CAN network will become insufficient in the near future. Although an integrated architecture can limit the requirement for further increases in the number of ECUs through the physical integration of functions, higher bandwidth demands are inevitable with the extending range of electronics in cars.

Investigation of Authentic CAN Communication Service

An important part of the validation activities has been the analysis of the CAN emulation's ability to provide significant properties (message ordering, message permanence, cancelability, transmission latencies) of a physical CAN network. Since the correctness of legacy applications can depend on these properties, their establishment is a prerequisite for the reuse of CAN legacy applications in a time-triggered environment without redevelopment and retesting efforts.

Investigation of Extended CAN Communication Service

An extended CAN communication service aims at newly developed CAN applications. These applications can benefit from higher bandwidths (> 1 Mbps) and additional services (e.g., global time, membership information) that are not provided by the CAN protocol [Bosch, 1991]. We will demonstrate the exceeding of CAN bandwidth limitations and describe the limits of the implementation of the CAN emulation with respect to bandwidths and upper bounds for transmission latencies.

Furthermore, the absence of contention between the traffic of different nodes in the CAN emulation decouples the temporal behavior of CAN message transmissions. Based on these considerations, we evaluate the complexity in designing applications that employ the extended CAN communication service, in relation to a conventional CAN system.

6.2   Transmission Latencies

The time-triggered communication protocol underlying the CAN emulation uses TDMA for media access control, i.e. it statically divides the channel capacity into a number of slots and assigns a unique slot to every node. The communication activities of every node are controlled by a time-triggered communication schedule, which specifies at what global points in time nodes send and receive messages. The time-triggered communication schedule also specifies the size and frequency of CAN slots, which are employed by the generic event service for the construction of event-triggered communication channels (ETCCs). Since ETCCs provide the foundation for the emulated CAN controller, the schedule also determines the transmission latencies of the emulated CAN communication service.

Schedule Parameters

The parameters of the communication schedule, which are significant for determining the latency of a CAN message transmission via an ETCC are summarized in Table 6.1.

Table 6.1.   Communication Schedule Parameters

Variable description	Variable	Remarks
number of nodes	n	$n \in \mathbb{N}$
number of TDMA rounds per cluster cycle	l	$l \in \mathbb{N}$
duration of node j's slot in TDMA round i	$s_{i,j}$	$1 \leqslant i \leqslant l, 1 \leqslant j \leqslant n$
data bytes for CAN in round i for node j	$r_{i,j}$	$1 \leqslant i \leqslant l, 1 \leqslant j \leqslant n$
duration of TDMA round i	d_i	$d_i = \sum_{j=1}^{n} s_{i,j}$

A sequence of sending slots, which allows every node in an ensemble of n nodes to send exactly once, is called a TDMA round. The sequence of the different TDMA rounds forms the cluster cycle and determines the periodicity of the time-triggered communication. We denote the number of TDMA rounds in this sequence with l. A statically defined duration d_i is associated with every TDMA round $i \in \{1,\dots,l\}$ of the cluster cycle. Hence, the duration of the cluster cycle is $\sum_{i=1}^{l}(d_i)$. For each TDMA round $i \in \{1,\dots,l\}$, we use the variables $s_{i,j}$ to specify the duration of the slot written by node j $(0 < j \leqslant n)$ within the TDMA round i. We assume that in all TDMA rounds the node index determines the temporal succession of the slots corresponding to the nodes, i.e. the following condition holds for any two nodes n_1, n_2 with corresponding slots s_{i,n_1}, s_{i,n_2} in any TDMA round i:

$$\forall i \in \{1,\dots,l\}, \forall n_1, n_2 \in \{1,\dots,n\}:\ n_1 < n_2 \Leftrightarrow \text{slot } s_{i,n_1} \text{ occurs before slot } s_{i,n_2}$$
$$(6.1)$$

The variables $s_{i,j}$ include the protocol overhead of the time-triggered communication protocol, e.g., CRC codes to detect channel faults and interframe gaps. The variables $r_{i,j}$ represent the number of data bytes used for CAN emulation by node j in round i. $r_{i,j}$ is a fraction of the effective data (excluding protocol overhead) communicated by node j in round i.

Worst-Case and Best-Case Latencies of Event Messages

Based on the parameters of the underlying time-triggered communication schedule (see Table 6.1), we can specify the worst-case latency for the transmission of a CAN message m via the ETCC at node k.

$$d_{m,k}^{\text{worst}} = \max_{r_1 \in \{1,\dots,l\}} \left(\sum_{j=k}^{n} s_{r_1,j} + \sum_{r=r_1+1}^{r_2-1} d_r + \sum_{j=1}^{k} s_{r_2,j} \,\middle|\, r_2 = \min_{i \in \mathbb{N}} \left(\sum_{j=r_1}^{i} r_{1+(j-1) \bmod l,k} > d_m^{\text{trans}} \right) \right)$$

d_m^{trans} denotes the length of the extended CAN messages in bytes. It depends on the number of effective data bytes in the CAN messages, the type of CAN message (basic or extended), and the overhead of the control bits and the timestamp.

$$d_m^{\text{trans}} = \begin{cases} \#\text{ effective data bytes} + 9 & \text{if } m \text{ is an extended CAN message} \\ \#\text{ effective data bytes} + 7 & \text{otherwise} \end{cases} \quad (6.2)$$

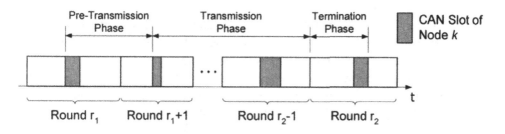

Figure 6.2. Phases of a CAN Message Transmission via an ETCC

The transmission of a CAN message via an ETCC can be decomposed into three phases, namely the pre-transmission phase, the transmission phase, and the termination phase (see Figure 6.2). These phases are represented by the three subtotals in the formula for $d_{m,k}^{\text{worst}}$. The pre-transmission phase corresponds to the sampling nature of the time-triggered transport service underlying the ETCC. A packet of a fragmented CAN message cannot be disseminated before a CAN slot occurs according to the time-triggered communication schedule. In the worst-case a transmission is requested immediately after a CAN slot, thereby causing a delay of an entire TDMA round for the transmission start of the CAN message. Similarly, a system that samples a variable will show a delay of a single period in case the variable changes its value immediately after a sampling point. During the transmission phase, the packets of the fragmented CAN message are communicated. The termination phase is the duration from the beginning of the TDMA round in which the last packet of a CAN message is communicated to the end of the CAN slot in this final TDMA round. r_1 denotes the round in which the transmission has been requested, i.e. the number of communication rounds since the system startup. r_2 ($r_2 > r_1$) is the round in which the CAN transmission finishes. It results from the size of the CAN slots in the rounds succeeding r_1. In the formula for $d_{m,k}^{\text{worst}}$, r_1 is chosen to maximize the resulting transmission latency, in order to obtain the worst-case transmission latency. Due to the periodic communication behavior, which is determined by the length of cluster cycle in TDMA rounds l, only values of $r_1 \in \{1, \ldots, l\}$ need to be considered.

The best-case transmission latency for a CAN message dissemination via an ETCC requires the CAN slot to occur immediately after the transmission request. In this case the pre-transmission phase has a length of zero.

$$d_{m,k}^{\text{best}} = \min_{r_1 \in \{1,\dots,l\}} \left(\sum_{r=r_1+1}^{r_2-1} d_r + \sum_{j=1}^{k} s_{r_2,j} \ \Big| \ r_2 = \min_{i \in \mathbb{N}} \left(\sum_{j=r_1}^{i} r_{1+(j-1)} \bmod l, k > d_m^{\text{trans}} \right) \right)$$

Note, that the calculation of the best-case transmission latency chooses the variable r_1 in order to minimize the resulting transmission latency. Similarly to the calculation of the worst-case transmission latency, only values of $r_1 \in \{1,\dots,l\}$ need to be considered.

The formulas for the calculation of $d_{m,k}^{\text{worst}}$ and $d_{m,k}^{\text{best}}$ specify the transmission latencies of an ETCC based on the timing behavior of the underlying time-triggered transport protocol. When multiple message streams compete for access to an ETCC at a node, queuing delays and processing overhead of the emulated CAN controller must be taken into account. The worst-case transmission latency is increased by the worst-case queuing delay at the sender's outgoing queue and the worst-case execution time of the software implementing the CAN controller emulation.

Latencies for Uniform Communication Schedules

We can also consider the special case of a cluster cycle consisting of equally sized TDMA rounds, which have an identical structure with respect to CAN communication, i.e. the placement and length of CAN slots is identical within all TDMA rounds. Based on these restrictions, we can provide a simplified version for the worst-case and best-case ETCC transmission latencies.

$$
\begin{aligned}
d_{m,k}^{\text{worst}} &= s_{0,k} + \left\lceil \frac{d_m^{trans}}{r_{0,k}} \right\rceil \cdot d_0 \\
d_{m,k}^{\text{best}} &= s_{0,k} + \left(\left\lceil \frac{d_m^{trans}}{r_{0,k}} \right\rceil - 1 \right) \cdot d_0
\end{aligned}
\tag{6.3}
$$

Timing Parameters in Prototype Implementation

For the implementation of CAN communication services in the TTA, we have used a cluster of TTP monitoring nodes [TTTech, 2002a] interconnected by a redundant 25 Mbps TTP/C network. For the C2 communication controller [TTTech, 2002b] deployed in the TTP monitoring nodes, the duration of a node j's slot in TDMA round i can be calculated as:

$$s_{i,j} = \left(\underbrace{\left\lceil \frac{4 \cdot d_{\text{corr\_max}} + t_{i,j} \cdot 320\,\text{ns} + d_{\text{proctime}}}{d_{\text{macrotick}}} \right\rceil + 1}_{\text{transmission phase}} + \underbrace{\left\lceil \frac{43\,\mu s}{d_{\text{macrotick}}} \right\rceil + 1}_{\text{inter frame gap}} \right) \cdot d_{\text{macrotick}}$$

The transmission duration $s_{i,j}$ incorporates both the sender node's transmission phase and the inter frame gap. It depends on the parameters contained in Table 6.2. The parameter d_{proctime} represents the time required for executing the C2 protocol code. It results from the clock frequency of the C2 controller and the number of instructions that must be executed. The delay correction d_{corr_max} depends on the propagation delay of the channel. The precision Π is determined by the skew of the controller clocks. $d_{macrotick}$ is the macrotick length of the global time base and must be at least the precision Π.

Table 6.2. Timing Paramters of C2 Communication Controller

Parameter	Value	Remarks
$d_{proctime}$	$7\,\mu s$	time for protocol execution
d_{corr_max}	$>1\,\mu s$	delay correction (depends on propagation delay)
Π	900 ns	precision
$d_{macrotick}$	$>\Pi$	length of a controller macrotick

For the determination of the parameters $t_{i,j}$, which denote the data bytes for CAN in round i for node j, we require an actual communication schedule. Figure 6.3

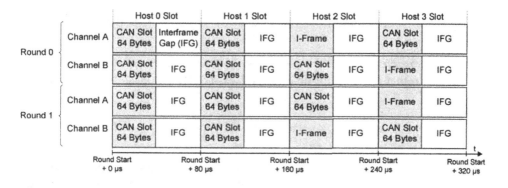

Figure 6.3. Communication Schedule with CAN Slots

depicts such a communication schedule, which provides CAN slots for four nodes with a TDMA round length of $320\,\mu s$. This communication schedule has also been employed for the measurements of the CAN emulation, which will be presented in Section 6.4.

6.3 Input Message Sets

This section presents the message sets that have been used during the validation activities as inputs for the CAN emulation on top of TTP/C and a simulation of a conventional CAN network. We will also present the underlying message model, which describes the temporal behavior of message transmission requests via an a priori known minimum interarrival time and a random duration modeled by a stochastic variable.

Message Model

In our message model, the dissemination of a message m is repeatedly requested at points in time $\rho_{k,m} \in \mathbb{R}^+$ ($k \in \mathbb{N}$), where $\rho_{k,m}$ are stochastic variables. Every message m is characterized by two parameters, an interarrival time $d_m \in \mathbb{R}^+$ and random intervals $\delta_{k,m} \in \mathbb{R}^+$.

$$\forall k \in \mathbb{N}: \quad \rho_{k+1,m} - \rho_{k,m} = d_m + \delta_{k,m} \tag{6.4}$$

d_m specifies an a priori known minimum interval of time between two transmission requests of m. The stochastic variables $\delta_{k,m}$ cover the random part in the time interval between two transmission requests of m. For a particular message m, all stochastic variables $\delta_{k,m}$ possess the same distribution function δ_m, i.e. $\delta_{k,m} \sim \delta_m$.

The two message parameters d_m and δ_m employed in this message model allow to distinguish between three fundamental message types:

- A *periodic message* has a constant time interval between successive message transmission requests.

$$m \text{ perodic} \quad \leftrightarrow \quad (\forall k \; \delta_{k,m} = 0) \; \wedge \; (d_m \in \mathbb{R} > 0) \tag{6.5}$$

- For a *sporadic message* the transmission request times are not known, but it is known that a minimum time interval exists between successive transmission requests.

$$m \text{ sporadic} \quad \leftrightarrow \quad (\forall k \; \delta_{k,m} \sim \delta_m) \; \wedge \; (d_m \in \mathbb{R} > 0) \tag{6.6}$$

- For an *aperiodic message* neither the message transmission request times are known nor a minimum time interval between successive transmission requests.

$$m \text{ aperiodic} \quad \leftrightarrow \quad (\forall k \; \delta_{k,m} \sim \delta_m) \; \wedge \; (d_m = 0) \tag{6.7}$$

Synthetic Message Sets

The synthetic message sets consist of CAN messages complying with the extended format [Bosch, 1991], the layout of which is depicted in Figure 6.4. An extended CAN message contains 67 control bits and between 0 and 8 bytes of effective data. Consequently, a complete CAN message has a length between 67 and 131 bits. In addition, there is a data dependent overhead for bit stuffing to prevent more than five consecutive bits of the same polarity. In CAN, six consecutive bits of the same polarity are used for error and protocol control signaling.

We have employed two groups of input message sets. One group consists of sporadic messages, a second one uses aperiodic messages. In both groups, we have specified maximum bandwidth values in order to determine the effects of

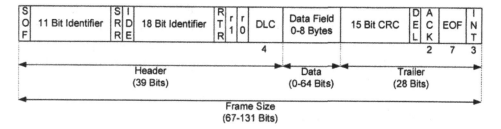

Figure 6.4. Layout of an Extended Format CAN Message

different message loads on the communication system. We have used the following expression for the determination of the bandwidth usage of a message m:

$$bandwidth(m) = \frac{b_m}{d_m + \mathbb{E}\left[\delta_m\right]} \tag{6.8}$$

where d_m denotes the minimum interarrival time of transmission request of message m. δ_m is the distribution function of the stochastic variables $\delta_{k,m}$ that represent the random intervals between transmission requests. b_m is the length of message m in bits. For our synthetic message sets $b_m = 99$ **bits,** due to the use of extended format CAN messages with 4 data bytes. We do not consider bit stuffing, because the additional overhead of bit stuffing is data dependent and mechanisms have been devised to significantly reduce the number of stuffing bits in CAN [Nolte et al., 2002].

We use the assumption of a uniform distribution for the lengths of random intervals $\delta_{k,m}$ of message transmission requests. For a particular message m, we consider all random intervals $\delta_{k,m}$ to possess the same distribution function $U(0, u_m)$.

$$\delta_{k,m} \sim \delta_m = U(0, u_m) \tag{6.9}$$

This leads to the following sum for the bandwidth usage of a message set M:

$$bandwidth(M) = \sum_{m \in M} \frac{99}{d_m + 0.5 \cdot u_m} \tag{6.10}$$

Based on this formula for the calculation of the bandwidth usage of a message set, we have constructed traffic patterns with sporadic and aperiodic messages and bandwidth usages of 500kbps, 1 Mbps, 2 Mbps, and 4 Mbps. We have employed a fixed number of 10 messages for the 500kbps pattern, subsequently doubling the number of messages along with doubling the bandwidth limit. Hence, we have constructed a maximum of 80 messages for the 4 Mbps traffic pattern.

For the aperiodic message sets, we have started with an upper bound $u_m = 1$ **ms** for the random interval length and added a linearly increasing summand until reaching the bandwidth limit with the predefined number of messages (10, 20, 40 and 80 messages). For the sporadic messages sets, the random interval length starts at $u_m = 500\,\mu s$, the initial minimum interarrival time d_m is $250\,\mu s$. Both the random interval length and the minimum interarrival time of subsequent messages are increased with a linearly increasing summand until reaching the bandwidth limit with the predefined number of messages.

Automotive Message Sets

Three prevalent types of networks can be found in modern cars: powertrain, body and comfort, and infotainment networks [Leen and Heffernan, 2002]. Infotainment networks provide the communication infrastructure for mobile entertainment and communication services. Body and comfort networks control seat and window movement and other non-critical user interfaces. Powertrain networks interconnect ECUs for engine management, anti-lock braking (ABS), electronic stability programs (ESP) [Bosch, 1998], transmission control, cruise control, and traction control. According to the SAE classification, which is based on bit transfer rates, powertrain networks correspond to class C (high speed network with a bandwidth between 125kbps and 1 Mbps) [Leen et al., 1999].

The traffic patterns from the real-world automotive application originate from a powertrain network and consist of 102 periodic messages. The message periods range from 3.3 ms to 1 s, the number of data bytes is between 2 and 8 bytes. Messages comply with the standard CAN format and contain 47 control bits, thereby resulting in a total message size between 47 and 111 bits. The overall network bandwidth required for the exchange of these messages is 300kbps.

Message Transmission Request Tables

We have constructed an offline tool, which creates transmission request tables based on the traffic patterns with periodic, sporadic, and aperiodic messages. The offline tool uses a random number generator for determining the lengths of the uniformly distributed random intervals in the aperiodic and sporadic transmission requests. For every node, a dedicated table specifies the global points in time for message transmission requests along with the corresponding message identifiers and message lengths. These tables control the message transmission behavior of the measurement and simulation activities. The reason for using request tables with absolute transmission times instead of directly employing the synthetic and automotive traffic patterns is the reduction of the run-time overhead and the reproducibility of simulation and measurement results. In addition, this approach eases the comparison of data collected via simulation and measurement runs.

6.4   Simulations and Measurements

We have compared a simulation of a conventional CAN network and measurements of the CAN emulation prototype implementation. This section describes the corresponding simulation and measurement frameworks and presents a selection of the measurement results. A detailed description of the data collected during the measurement and simulation runs can be found in [Obermaisser, 2004a].

Measurement Framework

The measurement framework for the validation of the event-triggered services and the CAN emulation employs the setup developed in the CAN emulation prototype implementation (see Section 5.5). A distributed measurement application uses the off-line computed message transmission request tables as inputs for the CAN emulation. The measurement application at every sender node exploits the services of the emulated CAN communication service and requests message transmissions at the points in time specified in the request table (see Figure 6.5). The table also determines the length and identifier of each transmitted message. The data area of the CAN message contains a message index, which uniquely identifies a particular message transmission request along with the node from which the message originated. The message index is required for the validation of the protocol emulation.

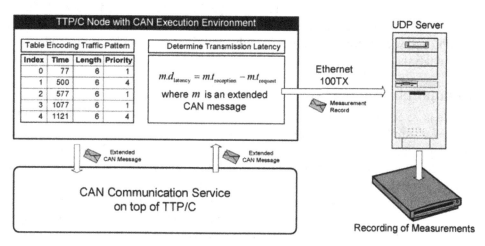

Figure 6.5. Measurement Framework

In order to allow protocol emulation, the CAN emulation extends every CAN message with a timestamp encoding the time $m.t_{request}$ of the transmission request. For the measurement activities, we use this timestamp contained in an extended CAN message to calculate message transmission latencies. After the reception of a CAN message m, the measurement application stores the current value of the global time in a variable $m.t_{reception}$ and calculates the transmission latency $m.d_{latency}$ of the message m:

$$m.d_{latency} = m.t_{reception} - m.t_{request} \qquad (6.11)$$

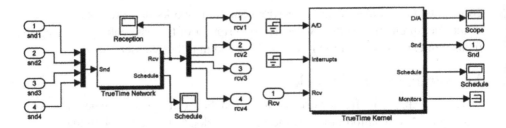

Figure 6.6. MATLAB /Simulink Models for Node (left) and Network (right)

The transmission latency $m.d_{\text{latency}}$ incorporates queuing delays in the CAN emulation at the sender, latencies of the underlying network and execution times of the CAN middleware. A measurement record is constructed with the index of the sending TTP/C node, the sequence number of the message, the reception time $m.t_{\text{reception}}$, and the transmission latency $m.d_{\text{latency}}$.

$$< \text{sender node, message sequence number, } m.t_{\text{reception}}, \; m.d_{\text{latency}} >$$

The measurement record is stored in a UDP packet and transferred to a workstation that executes a UDP server. The workstation collects the measurement records from TTP/C nodes and stores them into a dedicated file for each observing node for a later analysis.

Simulation Framework

We have employed a framework based on the MATLAB/Simulink toolbox TRUE-TIME for simulating the behavior of a conventional CAN network, when provided with a particular message pattern as input. TRUETIME [Cervin, 2000; Henriksson et al., 2002] is a MATLAB/Simulink-based simulation toolbox for real-time control systems. TRUETIME supports the simulation of the temporal behavior of tasks in a host computer, as well the simulation of the timing behavior of communication networks. For this purpose, it offers two Simulink blocks: a computer block and a network block. The blocks are variable-step, discrete, MATLAB S functions written in C++. The computer block S-function simulates a host computer with a flexible real-time kernel and user-defined tasks. Every task is associated with code (e.g., C functions), which is executed during the simulation. The network block operates event-driven and is triggered by messages entering or leaving the network. The network block is parameterized with the medium access control protocol (CSMA/CD, CSMA/CA, round robin, FDMA, or TDMA) and the transmission rate. A send queue is used to hold all messages currently enqueued in the network.

While TRUETIME has primarily been designed for analyzing the effects of timing non-determinism on control performance, the high flexibility of the computer block and the support for the CAN media access control protocol (CSMA/CA) make this tool well-suited for simulating a conventional CAN system. We use the

TRUETIME computer and network blocks (see Figure 6.6) to model a CAN system consisting of four nodes. Every node employs a TRUETIME computer block that is connected to the network block modeling the CAN bus. In every node, a task is executed that transmits messages according to a message transmission request table as described in Section 6.3. At the points in time specified in this table, the task passes CAN messages to the TRUETIME network. The CAN message is assigned the priority and length as specified in the table. The data area contains the point in time of the message transmission request and a unique index to identify the message.

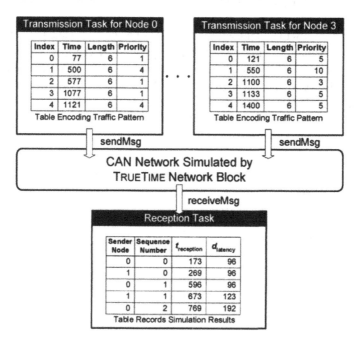

Transmission Task for Node 0

Index	Time	Length	Priority
0	77	6	1
1	500	6	4
2	577	6	1
3	1077	6	1
4	1121	6	4

Table Encoding Traffic Pattern

Transmission Task for Node 3

Index	Time	Length	Priority
0	121	6	5
1	550	6	10
2	1100	6	3
3	1133	6	5
4	1400	6	5

Table Encoding Traffic Pattern

sendMsg   sendMsg

CAN Network Simulated by
TRUETIME Network Block

receiveMsg

Reception Task

Sender Node	Sequence Number	$t_{reception}$	$d_{latency}$
0	0	173	96
1	0	269	96
0	1	596	96
1	1	673	123
0	2	769	192

Table Records Simulation Results

Figure 6.7. Simulation Tasks

One of the nodes also hosts a reception task. The reception task is an interrupt handler that is triggered by message receptions. This task retrieves the CAN message from the TRUETIME network and calculates the transmission latency from the timestamp contained in the message and the current simulation time. The determined transmission latency is written into a file for a later analysis. The interplay between the transmission and reception tasks is visualized in Figure 6.7.

Results for Synthetic Message Sets

We have used the message sets described in Section 6.3 as inputs for both the MATLAB/Simulink-based simulation of a physical CAN network and the implementation of the CAN emulation. Figures 6.8–6.10 present the results of the measurement and simulation runs for the message sets with sporadic transmission requests. The figures contain diagrams with the distributions of the observed message transmission latencies. The transmission latencies are distinguished along the x-axis. The y-axis represents the number of messages observed with a particular transmission latency. We have chosen a logarithmic scaling of the y-axis in order to emphasize rare latency values in the diagrams.

A CAN network with a bandwidth of 1 Mbps has been modeled in the simulation, since 1 Mbps is the maximum bandwidth supported by the CAN protocol. Consequently, only input traffic with a bandwidth limit of 500 kbps or 1 Mbps was fed into the simulation. For the traffic patterns with 2 Mbps we provide only measurement results from the CAN emulation.

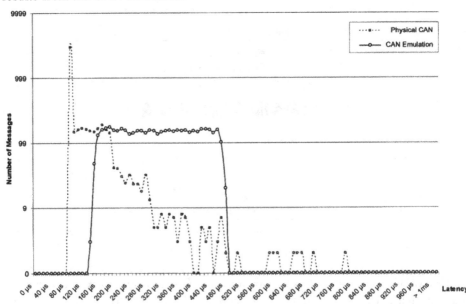

Figure 6.8. Measurement and Simulation Results (Sporadic Traffic, 500 kbps): *For the 500 kbps message sets, the CAN emulation (solid line) and the physical CAN network (dashed line) offer similar transmission latencies. The physical CAN network provides lower best-case latencies (99 μs). The CAN emulation, on the other hand, possesses higher best-case latencies (147 μs), but is superior with respect to the worst-case behavior. No transmission latency higher than 490 μs has been observed.*

The measurement and simulation results for the sporadic traffic patterns with 500 kbps are depicted in Figure 6.8. The observed transmission latencies of the CAN emulation (solid line) are uniformly distributed between 147 μs and 490 μs. At the overall bandwidth consumption of 500 kbps by CAN messages, the accumulation of CAN message transmission requests during a TDMA round does not exceed the available bandwidth of a node's CAN slot. Consequently, the CAN emulation does not perform a fragmentation of CAN messages. The best-case latency of **147 μs** results from the execution time of the CAN emulation middleware and the transmission time of a CAN message via the node's CAN slot. The best-case latency occurs, when a transmission request occurs prior to the corresponding CAN slot. The worst-case latency (**490 μs**) is observed, when a transmission request occurs after the node's CAN slot, thus inducing an additional delay of one TDMA round. In this case, the transmission latency is the sum of the TDMA round duration, the actual transmission time via the node's CAN slot, and the execution time of the CAN emulation middleware.

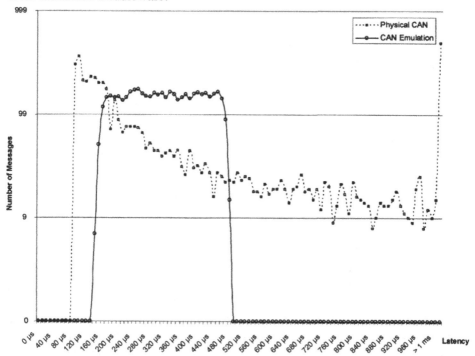

Figure 6.9. Measurement and Simulation Results (Sporadic Traffic, 1 Mbps): *The transmission latencies observed in the CAN emulation (solid line) are uniformly distributed between **147 μs** and **490 μs**. Physical CAN (dashed line) exhibits a large variability of transmission latencies. 4.9% of message transmissions exhibit the best-case latency of **99 μs**. 10.4% of message transmissions exhibit latencies above 1 ms (peak of physical CAN latencies on right most side of the diagram).*

The dashed line in Figure 6.8 depicts the results of the simulation of a physical CAN network. On the physical CAN network, a large number of messages (53%) occur with the best-case latency of **99 μs**. The maximum observed latency for the sporadic message set with a bandwidth usage of 500 kbps has been **790 μs** in the simulation of the physical CAN network.

At the overall bandwidth consumption of 1 Mbps by CAN messages (see Figure 6.9), the accumulation of CAN message transmission requests during a TDMA round does not exceed the available bandwidth of a node's CAN slot. Consequently, the transmission latencies observed in the CAN emulation (solid line) are uniformly distributed between 147 μs and **490 μs**. The simulation of the physical CAN network (dashed line) exhibits a larger variability of transmission latencies. The transmission latencies of the physical CAN network, which is now fully utilized, range between 99 μs and **2720 μs**.

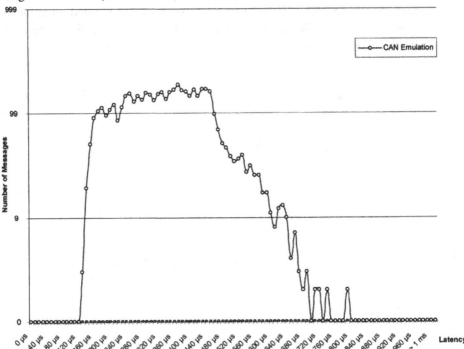

Figure 6.10.   Measurement and Simulation Results (Sporadic Traffic, 4 Mbps): *At the overall bandwidth consumption of 4 Mbps by CAN messages, transmission latencies vary between 147 μs and 796 μs. The larger worst-case latencies result from the fragmentation of messages through the CAN emulation middleware. Fragmentation is applied in those TDMA rounds, in which the accumulation of requested CAN message transmissions exceeds the available bandwidth of the node's CAN slot.*

Since conventional CAN networks do not support bandwidths above 1 Mbps, Figure 6.10 depicts only measurement results from the CAN emulation for the 4 Mbps message set. Worst-case transmission latencies are higher than for the 1 Mbps message set, because of intervals of time during which the rate of message transmission requests exceeds a node's bandwidth available through the underlying time-triggered communication schedule. In this case, message transmissions require multiple communication rounds. The worst-case latency for the 4 Mbps message set is **796 μs**.

Results for Automotive Message Sets

The traffic patterns from the automotive industry were used as inputs for both the simulation of a conventional CAN network and the CAN prototype emulation implementation. In the simulation, we have modeled a CAN network with a bandwidth of 500 kbps.

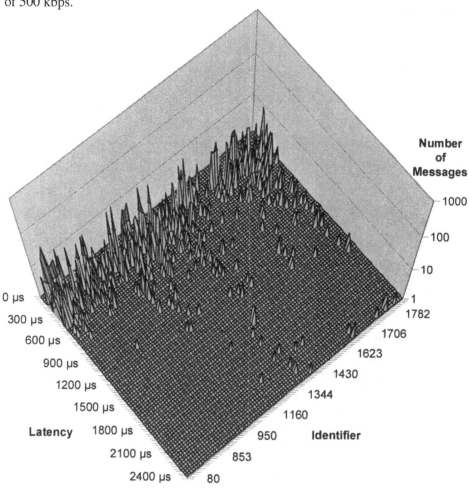

Figure 6.11. Simulation Results for Automotive Message Traffic (Logarithmic Scaling of z-axis)

The simulation results for the automotive traffic are depicted in Figure 6.11. The x-axis represents the message transmission latencies. The message identifiers are distinguished along the y-axis. These identifiers range from 80 to 2004 and denote the message priority. Larger CAN identifiers correspond to lower message priorities. The distance along the z-axis represents the number of messages with a given message priority and transmission latency. Figure 6.11 shows that high priority messages make up for a large amount of the overall bandwidth. The third of messages with the highest priority makes up for 49% of exchanged messages. The simulation results also demonstrate the high average performance of CAN. 97% of all message transmissions possess transmission latencies below 1 ms. However, transmission latencies vary considerably. The logarithmic scaling of the z-axis in Figure 6.11 emphasizes the rare cases, in which transmission latencies significantly differ from the average values.

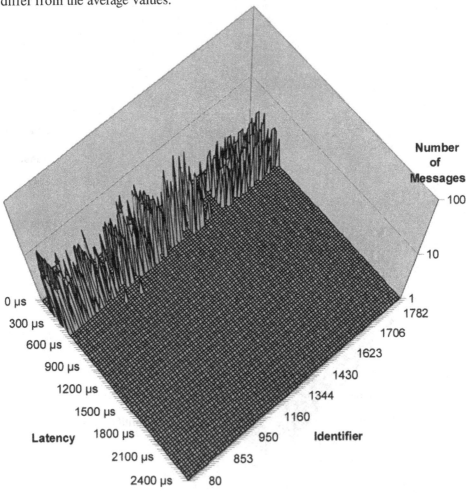

Figure 6.12. Measurement Results for Automotive Message Traffic (Logarithmic Scaling of z-axis)

Figure 6.12 depicts the measured transmission latencies for the automotive traffic in the CAN emulation implementation. The observed worst-case latency is **608 μs**, i.e. significantly lower compared to the **3165 μs** of the conventional CAN network. The best-case latency is **147 μs**. The average message transmission latency of the measurements is **323.51 μs**. An overview of the latencies observed in the simulation and measurements is contained in Table 6.3.

Table 6.3. Overview of Observed Latencies in Simulation and Emulation

	Best-Case	Worst-Case	Average	Variance
Simulation	126 μs	3165 μs	350.11 μs	78581.45
Emulation	147 μs	608 μs	323.51 μs	8371.96

6.5 Discussion of Authentic CAN Communication Service

The simulation and measurement results have demonstrated the ability of the CAN emulation to provide significant properties of a conventional CAN network. No differences with respect to message permanence, message ordering, and message cancelability have been observed. Furthermore, the CAN emulation and a physical CAN network exhibit similar transmission latencies. The ability to reproduce the transmission latencies of a conventional CAN network is determined by the frequency and size of communication slots dedicated to the CAN emulation.

Message Permanence and Message Ordering

The protocol emulation algorithm in the CAN prototype implementation reestablishes significant properties of a conventional CAN network. For every received CAN message, this algorithm determines the point in time at which the message becomes permanent, i.e. when it is known that all earlier messages would have arrived on a conventional CAN network. By determining message permanence for every received CAN message before exposing the message to the application, the protocol emulation algorithm also establishes the message ordering of a conventional CAN network.

We have performed the validation of this protocol emulation algorithm by including sequence numbers in the CAN messages that were transmitted via the emulated CAN communication service and the MATLAB/Simulink-based CAN simulation. The comparison of the observed sequence numbers has indicated no differences in the message ordering between the emulated CAN communication service and the simulation of a conventional CAN network.

Ability to Cancel Messages

Many existing CAN controllers (e.g., Intel i82527 [Intel Corporation, 1995]) allow to cancel transmission requests until the transmission of a message is actually started. The CAN emulation supports cancelability via explicit cancellation messages that inform nodes about the need to discard previously received messages. As cancellation messages are also subject to protocol emulation, they are ordered along with other CAN messages. A cancellation message only takes effect, if it occurs before the corresponding target message in the final message ordering. In this case, the cancellation would have occurred before the start of the message transmission on the conventional CAN network.

Transmission Latencies

In Section 5.3, we have identified different levels of authenticity for the reproduction of transmission latencies, three of which (L2–L4) are significant for the CAN emulation: minimum guaranteed transmission latencies of a conventional CAN network, transmission latencies of a CAN network in the presence of communication faults, and a best-effort strategy.

Level L2, i.e. the minimum guaranteed transmission latency of a conventional CAN network, imposes the lowest acceptable bounds for transmission latencies. Consequently, we focus on level L2 in the analysis of the transmission latencies. In a conventional CAN network, the minimum guaranteed transmission latency can be establishes for the highest priority message, since the highest priority message will always win the arbitration process. As described in Section 5.2, the upper bound for the transmission latency of the highest priority message h is:

$$R_h = J_h + \max_{\forall k \in lp(m)} (C_k) + C_h \qquad (6.12)$$

Consider for example, a CAN network with $\tau_{bit} = 2\,\mu s$, i.e. a bandwidth of 500 kbps. If extended format CAN messages with 4 data bytes are exchanged, then $C_m = 226\,\mu s$. If we abstract from the queuing jitter, we can establish the bound $R_h = 452\,\mu s$ for the maximum transmission latency of the highest priority message h.

In Section 6.2 we have derived a formula for the maximum transmission latencies of event messages on top of a time-triggered communication protocol. The maximum transmission latency for a message is a function of significant properties of the communication controller and the communication schedule of the underlying time-triggered communication system. Section 6.2 describes the general case with an arbitrary structure of cluster cycles and the special case of a cluster cycle consisting of equally sized TDMA rounds. In the latter case, the worst-case delay $d_{m,k}^{worst}$ of the communication service for message m from node k is:

$$d_{m,k}^{worst} = s_k + \left\lceil \frac{d_m^{trans}}{r_k} \right\rceil \cdot d, \qquad (6.13)$$

where d_m^{trans} denotes the length of the extended CAN messages in bytes. s_k represents the length of node k's slot, d represents the length of a TDMA round ($d = \sum_i s_i$), and r_k denotes the number of bytes available for CAN communication at node k.

For the CAN communication service, we must also consider delays due to local contention at a node. Messages are fragmented over multiple TDMA rounds, if applications within a node request more messages than can be sent via the time-triggered communication protocol. This situation leads to the accumulation of messages in outgoing message queues, when the overall sum of message lengths exceeds the node's slot size in the following TDMA round. However, the highest priority message h will never be subject to fragmentation, if the size of the node's slot is larger or equal to the message length of h. Hence, the value of $d_{h,k}^{\text{worst}}$ determines the ability of the CAN communication service to provide the guaranteed maximum latencies of a conventional CAN network (L2), which is necessary for the highest priority message.

For the measurements of the CAN prototype implementation, we have employed a communication schedule with four nodes. Each node k has been assigned a slot with 64 bytes of data (i.e. $r_k = 64$) and a length $s_k = 80\,\mu s$. Consequently, the round length is $d = 320\,\mu s$. Based on these schedule parameters, the maximum transmission latency $d_{m,k}^{\text{worst}}$ of a CAN message m sent via the time-triggered transport protocol is $d_{m,k}^{\text{worst}} = 400\,\mu s$. For the highest priority message h, no additional delay occurs through other messages, which locally compete with h for transmission. Since every node is assigned 64 bytes, it is guaranteed that the highest priority message is completely transmitted within the following TDMA round, i.e. without fragmentation. Of course, the actual transmission latency is further increased by the execution time of the middleware services, in addition to $d_{m,k}^{\text{worst}}$. The latency measurements described in Section 6.4 also include the overhead that is imposed by the middleware services. In these measurements, a maximum latency of $479\,\mu s$ has been observed for the highest priority message. While this bound would be sufficient for providing the maximum guaranteed latency of a 250 kbps CAN network, this value is slightly larger than the bound of a 500 kbps CAN network. Nevertheless, the CAN prototype implementation can accommodate to different underlying time-triggered communication schedules. For example, a faster time-triggered communication controller would permit a reduction of the round length, thereby allowing the provision of latency guarantees in equivalence to conventional CAN with bandwidths of 500 kbps or 1 Mbps.

If the reproduction of transmission latencies in the presence of faults is sufficient, the duration of inaccessibility times determines the acceptable values for $d_{m,k}^{\text{worst}}$, instead of R_h. The maximum latency of $479\,\mu s$ observed during the measurements of the CAN emulation is significantly below the possible inaccessibility time of 2.2 ms in a 1 Mbps CAN network. Hence, the CAN emulation with the employed underlying communication schedule permits the emulation of a 1 Mbps CAN network with latency reproduction level L3.

It can be concluded, that the key element for establishing a certain level of communication latencies for a CAN communication service on top of a time-triggered communication protocol is the structure of the time-triggered communication schedule. Emulated CAN communication latencies can be controlled via the round lengths and the number of bytes dedicated to the emulated CAN communication. In general, relaxed requirements with respect to transmission latency guarantees allow to increase round lengths or to decrease the number of bytes dedicated to the emulated CAN communication service.

Application Interface

The CAN emulation establishes the programming interface of a conventional CAN controller by providing the controller's register set. In the CAN prototype implementation, we have implemented the register interfaces of the Intel i82527 and the Philips SJA1000. We have implemented sample applications for these two CAN controllers for testing the programming interfaces. For the SJA1000 emulation, we have executed the test application both in the CAN emulation and within a physical CAN node that is equipped with a standard SJA1000 controller.

6.6   Discussion of Extended CAN Communication Service

The extended application interface has been designed for newly developed CAN applications, i.e. CAN applications that are not bound to a legacy CAN controller. The extended application interface offers additional services, namely access to the global time of TTP/C and a membership service. In addition, the extended CAN application interface separates the communication activities of different nodes, thereby reducing the complexity in reasoning about the temporal behavior of message exchanges.

Temporal Behavior

In a conventional CAN system, the temporal behavior of a message transmission is controlled via a message identifier, which denotes the priority of the message in relation to other messages. The major difficulty in using this priority-based mechanism is the inability to argue locally about the effects of the selection of a particular identifier on the temporal behavior of a message transmission. Except for the highest priority message, the actual transmission latency of a CAN message depends on the higher priority messages competing for network access. Due to this global contention of a CAN network, any statement about temporal bounds of the transmission latency for a message other than the one with the highest priority, must be based on restrictions or assumptions about the transmission behavior of other nodes. The CAN protocol [Bosch, 1991] does not provide mechanisms to enforce such restrictions regarding the rate or timing of message transmissions of nodes.

The CAN communication service implemented on top of TTP/C helps in managing complexity by separating the communication activities at the level of the communication system. The temporal behavior of a message transmission depends only on the message transmissions occurring at the same node, i.e. the temporal behavior of a message transmission is independent of the transmission requests at other nodes. Unlike the global contention scheme of a conventional CAN system, the local contention of the CAN emulation allows to argue about the correct temporal behavior of a message transmission solely based on considerations about local message transmission requests.

Exceeding of CAN Limitations

The arbitration mechanism of CAN requires bits to stabilize on the channel and limits the maximum bandwidth to 1 Mbps at a network length of 40m. The bit length must be at least as large as the propagation delay.

The measurement results in Section 6.4 demonstrate the ability of the CAN emulation to handle bandwidths that exceed 1 Mbps. For a 2 Mbps message set, a maximum transmission latency of $680 \mu s$ has been observed. At 4 Mbps all messages were received within 1 ms.

6.7   Solving of Dependability Problems of the CAN Protocol

The CAN emulation makes existing legacy CAN applications more dependable through the fault-tolerance mechanisms of the underlying TTP/C protocol. For newly developed CAN applications, the CAN emulation helps in managing the complexity of establishing dependability. The fault-tolerance mechanisms of the time-triggered subsystem are provided transparently to applications.

The TTP/C protocol employs two replicated communication channels, thereby allowing to tolerate a failure of a single communication channel without any impact on the time-triggered communication service. The ability to tolerate the failure of a single channel also applies to the event-triggered CAN communication, as CAN communication is layered on top of the time-triggered communication services.

Fault-Tolerant Atomic Broadcast

The CAN protocol does not provide a consistent view of every transmitted message, in case a fault hits the last two bits of a message's seven bit end-of-frame delimiter [Rufino et al., 1998]. Existing solutions to this problem involve either additional hardware (e.g., shadow retransmitter [Livani, 1999]), or higher-level protocols with additional latencies and communication load (e.g., Eager-Diffusion based protocol for CAN [Rufino et al., 1998]).

The CAN emulation provides a fault-tolerant atomic broadcast through the underlying TTP/C protocol for failures specified in the fault hypothesis of the TTA [Bauer et al., 2001]. This fault hypothesis contains the assumption that only one node of a TTA cluster becomes faulty every TDMA round. A further node may become faulty only after the previously faulty node has shut down or operates correctly again.

Handling of Babbling Idiot Failures

A CAN-based application exploiting the services of the CAN emulation cannot block applications in other nodes from accessing the emulated CAN communication service. As the CAN emulation builds on top of the communication service of the TTA, the error containment mechanisms of the TTA [Kopetz, 2003] also apply to the CAN emulation. Furthermore, we provide separate incoming message queues for different ETCCs, i.e. separate queues for different sender tasks. A sender violating its interarrival time specification is likely to produce more messages than can be processed by receivers. These conditions can cause an accumulation of messages in incoming message queues and lead to message omissions. Due to the separation of incoming message queues, such a faulty sender cannot block the queuing capacities for messages from other senders.

No Change in Timing Behavior through Faults

The CAN protocol tolerates transient communication failures via message retransmissions. However, the retransmission mechanism results in increased latencies under the occurrence of faults, which is undesirable for jitter sensitive applications.

The CAN emulation tolerates failures of a communication channel via replication of the underlying communication channel. Redundant channels prevent an effect on the temporal behavior of the communication system in case a fault hits only a single communication channel.

Masquerading Failure

Masquerading is defined as the sending or receiving of messages using the identity of another sender without authority [Coulouris et al., 1994]. Consequently, even an external observer cannot identify the faulty sender. Such a forged message identifier can have a significant impact on the application. Figure 6.13 depicts this scenario. The faulty node with identifier 1 sends a message to all other nodes and it pretends to be node with identifier 5.

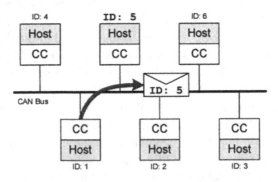

Figure 6.13.   Masquerading Failure in CAN

The extended CAN communication service of the integrated architecture prevents masquerading failures by using separate incoming message queues for different senders. In the example scenario of Figure 6.13, the CAN message from the faulty sender (identifier 1) is placed in a dedicated incoming message queue associated to this sender, thereby overcoming the diagnostic deficiency.

Chapter 7

CONCLUSION

The main contribution of this book is the development of a generic system architecture for the integration of the time-triggered and event-triggered control paradigms. This integrated architecture supports both time-triggered and event-triggered computational and communication activities. Thereby, a time-triggered and an event-triggered subsystem can coexist on a single, shared distributed computing platform. The application tasks executing in these subsystems adhere to different models of computation. While the time-triggered subsystem supports the time-triggered model of computation, the event-triggered subsystem is designed for client/server and event-based computing. This coexistence makes the proposed architecture suitable for mixed-criticality and legacy integration. Safety-critical time-triggered applications coexist with event-triggered legacy applications and newly developed, non-critical event-triggered applications.

Our starting-point is a time-triggered architecture, for which we assume a set of four fundamental, basic services: a predictable, fault-tolerant transport service, clock synchronization, error containment, and a membership service. The basic services provide the foundation for the time-triggered subsystem, and for higher-level architectural services, as required by applications in the event-triggered subsystem. The higher-level services include an event-triggered transport service, membership information for tasks in the event-triggered subsystem, gateway services, and additional error containment mechanisms for faults in the event-triggered subsystem. The additional error containment mechanisms are inter- and inner-component partitioning between tasks in the event-triggered subsystem, as well as between tasks in the event-triggered and time-triggered subsystems. The primary goal of the error containment mechanisms is the prevention of error propagation from non-safety critical subsystems to subsystems of higher criticality.

Through the distinction between basic and higher-level services and the strict separation of application functionality from generic architectural services, existing validation and certification results of applications and basic services are not invalidated through the addition of the event-triggered higher-level communication services and corresponding applications to a time-triggered system.

Varying Rigidity of Temporal Specifications. A major difference between applications in the time-triggered and event-triggered subsystems is the rigidity of the temporal specification of communication and computational activities. The time-triggered transport service employed by the time-triggered subsystem performs communication activities at predetermined, global points in time. In addition, tasks in the time-triggered subsystem possess deterministically known execution times. In contrast, the event-triggered transport service of the event-triggered subsystem must handle on-demand communication activities at a priori unknown points in time. In general, only probabilistic knowledge about the temporal behavior of tasks in the event-triggered subsystem is available via interarrival and service time distributions. Equally, knowledge about worst-case execution times of tasks in the event-triggered subsystem can be probabilistic or unavailable.

Consequently, the higher-level architectural services for the event-triggered subsystem are designed to handle imprecise temporal specifications, which are common to legacy applications and non safety-critical functions. The error detection and error containment mechanisms of the event-triggered subsystem build on top of the respective mechanisms of the time-triggered subsystem and handle the additional, occasional timing failures introduced by these imprecise temporal specifications.

The error containment mechanisms for the event-triggered subsystem focus on the prevention of error propagation from the sender to the receiver, since any error propagation in the opposite direction is prevented by the event-triggered communication service being an elementary interface.

Higher-Level Event-Triggered Services. Applications in the event-triggered subsystem are interconnected by an event-triggered communication service that is optimized for flexibility and resource efficiency. The event-triggered communication service is realized on top of the basic time-triggered communication service, thus providing a strict separation of basic and higher-level services. This approach avoids any complication of basic services and facilitates certification of the safety-critical time-triggered subsystem. Furthermore, the fault-tolerance mechanisms of the time-triggered subsystem transparently improve the fault-resilience of the event-triggered communication service. Errors covered by the error detection and error containment mechanisms of the time-triggered subsystem are handled once-and-for-all and need not be explicitly considered in the event-triggered subsystem.

The underlying time-triggered subsystem employs a sparse time base for communication activities at the time-triggered transport service. By mapping the event-triggered transport service to the underlying time-triggered communication system, event-triggered communication activities are also mapped to this sparse time base. The sparse time base enables the definition of a distributed state for both the time-triggered and event-triggered subsystems. The consistent distributed state simplifies the construction of membership information and the reintegration of both event-triggered and time-triggered subsystems (e.g., after transient failures).

CAN Emulation in the Time-Triggered Architecture. We have established a generic model of a second level communication controller for the establishment of an event-triggered communication service on top of a time-triggered transport protocol. The second level communication controller can be applied for a multitude of event-triggered communication protocols. Amongst its applications are a CAN communication service, a CORBA transport, and TCP/IP on top of a time-triggered protocol. For improving reusability and simplifying the adaptation to different platforms, the second level communication controller decomposes the problem of mapping the two control paradigms into three separate layers. A generic event service is responsible for mapping a state message interface into an even message interface. Protocol emulation reestablishes significant properties of the event-triggered communication protocol. The application interface provides a particular programming interface, e.g., for integrating legacy applications.

The CAN emulation in the Time-Triggered Architecture is an application of the generic system architecture for the integration of event-triggered and time-triggered services. The CAN emulation is of high industrial relevance, since CAN is widely used in present day cars. Despite the use of time-triggered architectures in future by-wire cars, CAN is likely to remain as a communication protocol for non-safety critical functions due to economic constraints. Even for safety-related functions, CAN-based legacy applications will not be replaced instantly. The CAN emulation enables the reuse of CAN-based legacy applications, thereby leveraging investments and avoiding redevelopment efforts. Physical CAN nodes are mapped into nodes of a time-triggered system and physical CAN networks are replaced by CAN overlay networks on top of a time-triggered communication service. This approach allows cost savings by reducing the overall number of ECUs in cars. The reduction of wiring and connectors eliminates potential faults and improves reliability.

The CAN application that is integrated into the time-triggered subsystem benefits from the properties of the underlying reliable time-triggered communication system. The emulation overcomes deficiencies of CAN like bandwidth limitations, inaccessibility times, and the lack of an atomic broadcast mechanism. This occurs at the protocol level without increasing application complexity.

Furthermore, we have demonstrated the ability to provide an authentic CAN communication service, as required for the integration of CAN-based legacy applications. We have identified significant properties of a conventional CAN network (ordering, permanence, cancelability, and latencies of messages). We have analytically established a relationship between transmission latencies of a CAN communication service and an underlying time-triggered communication schedule. A protocol emulation algorithm extends exchanged messages with additional temporal information, simulates the behavior of a conventional CAN network, and reestablishes the significant CAN properties. A comparison of measurements of the CAN emulation employing the protocol emulation algorithm with a conventional CAN network has indicated no differences with respect to the identified properties.

A Core Architecture for Integrated Modular Avionics.   An important factor for reusability and portability of application software is the availability of standards for platform-independent abstraction layers that hide the details of the underlying hardware (host processor, network) and software (operating system, middleware). In the avionics domain, ARINC 653 defines an Application Programming Interface (API) called APplication EXecutive (APEX) that represents such an abstraction layer. ARINC 653 specifies the software environment of ARINC 651 Integrated Modular Avionics (IMA) systems. It supports temporal and spatial partitioning by assigning a dedicated partition to each application function. ARINC 653 restricts the application software's accesses to the underlying platform to the APEX API. If applications do not by-bass the APEX functions, then error containment for the consequences of design faults in applications is guaranteed.

To construct an ARINC 651 compliant IMA architecture, the APEX API must be mapped to an underlying core architecture. Most importantly, the core architecture must provide the capabilities of supporting the services as specified by APEX. The system architecture proposed in this book is suited as a core architecture for IMA systems as it facilitates the establishment of the APEX API through the provision of error containment mechanisms and the availability of basic time-triggered architectural services in conjunction with higher-level event-triggered services. The time-triggered and event-triggered communication services of the system architecture are candidates for the two ARINC 653 communication modes, namely sampling mode for the exchange of messages containing state information, and queuing mode for messages with event information.

Event-triggered communication channels (ETCCs) and event-triggered virtual networks provide the foundation for queuing mode. When an APEX channel is mapped to an ETCC, applications can request the transmission of messages at arbitrary points in time. The provision of message queues facilitates the establishment of exactly-once processing semantics, as required for messages containing event information. The time-triggered communication service, on the other hand, performs periodic exchanges of state messages, thus allowing an implementation of sampling mode with a priori guarantees on the temporal accuracy of real-time images.

Furthermore, the proposed system architecture supports temporal and spatial partitioning as required for IMA systems. For both event-triggered and time-triggered communication, the architecture prevents error propagation via timing message failures and masquerading failures. At the component level, the proposed system architecture relies on the capabilities of the operating system. In the prototype implementation, the operating system RTAI Linux employs two-level scheduling to prevent timing failures of standard Linux tasks in user space from propagating into kernel space. For spatial inner-component partitioning, we apply a memory management unit (MMU) for controlling memory accesses of user space tasks.

References

Ademaj, A., Sivencrona, H., Bauer, G., and Torin, J. (2003). Evaluation of fault handling of the time-triggered architecture with bus and star topology. In *Proceedings of International Conference on Dependable Systems and Networks,* pages 123–132. Vienna University of Technology, Real-Time Systems Group.

Almeida, C. and Verissimo, P. (1998). Using light-weight groups to handle timing failures in quasi-synchronous systems. In *Proceedings of the 19th IEEE Real-Time Systems Symposium,* Madrid, Spain.

ARINC 429 (2001). *ARINC Specification 429: Digital Information Transfer System.* Aeronautical Radio, Inc., 2551 Riva Road, Annapolis, Maryland 21401.

ARINC 629 (1991). *ARINC Specification 629: Multi-Transmitter Data Bus – Part 1: Technical De-scription.* Aeronautical Radio, Inc., 2551 Riva Road, Annapolis, Maryland 21401.

ARINC 651 (1991). *ARINC Specification 651: Design Guide for Integrated Modular Avionics.* Aero-nautical Radio, Inc., 2551 Riva Road, Annapolis, Maryland 21401.

ARINC 653 (2003). *ARINC Specification 653-1 (Draft 3): Avionics Application Software Standard Interface.* Aeronautical Radio, Inc., 2551 Riva Road, Annapolis, Maryland 21401.

ARINC 659 (1993). *ARINC Specification 659: Backplane Data Bus.* Aeronautical Radio, Inc., 2551 Riva Road, Annapolis, Maryland 21401.

ARINC 664 – Part 1 (2002). *ARINC Specification 664: Aircraft Data Network Part 1 – Systems Concepts and Overview.* Aeronautical Radio, Inc., 2551 Riva Road, Annapolis, Maryland 21401.

ARINC 664 – Part 7 (2003). *ARINC Specification 664 (Draft): Aircraft Data Network Part 7 – Deterministic Networks.* Aeronautical Radio, Inc., 2551 Riva Road, Annapolis, Maryland 21401.

Audi AG, BMW AG, DaimlerChrysler AG, Motorola Inc., Volcano Communication Technologies AB, Volkswagen AG, and Volvo Car Corporation (1999). LIN specification and LIN press an-nouncement. *SAE World Congress Detroit.* www.lin-subbus.org.

Audsley, N.C., Bate, I.J., and Grigg, A. (1998). The role of timing analysis in the certification of IMA systems. *IEE Certification of Ground/Air Systems Seminar (Ref. No. 1998/255).* Dept. of Comput. Sci., York Univ., London, UK.

Avizienis, A. (1975). Fault-tolerance and fault-intolerance: Complementary approaches to reliable computing. In *Proceedings of the international conference on Reliable software,* pages 458–464.

Avizienis, A., Laprie, J.C., and Randell, B. (2001). Fundamental concepts of dependability. Research Report 01-145, LAAS-CNRS, Toulouse, France.

Bal, H.E., Steiner, J.G., and Tanenbaum, A.S. (1989). *Programming Languages for Distributed Sys-tems.* ACM Computer Surveys.

Barabanov, M. and Yodaiken, V. (1996). Real-time linux. *Linux Journal.*

Barborak, M., Dahbura, A., and Malek, M. (1993). The consensus problem in fault-tolerant computing. *ACM Computing Surveys (CSUR),* 25(2):171–220.

Bauer, G. and Kopetz, H. (2000). Transparent redundancy in the time-triggered architecture. In *Proceedings of the International Conference on Dependable Systems and Networks (DSN 2000), NY, USA, pages* 5–13.

Bauer, G., Kopetz, H., and Puschner, P. (2001). Assumption coverage under different failure modes in the time-triggered architecture. In *Proceedings of 8th IEEE International Conference on Emerging Technologies and Factory Automation,* volume 1, pages 333–341.

Bauer, G. and Paulitsch, M. (2000). An investigation of membership and clique avoidance in TTP/C. In *Proceedings of 19th IEEE Symposium on Reliable Distributed Systems,* pages 118–124, Nürnberg, Germany.

Beal, D., Bianchi, E., Dozio, L., Hughes, S., Mantegazza, P., and Papacharalambous, S. (2000). RTAI: Real-time application interface. *Linux Journal.*

Bellini, P., Mattolini, R., and Nesi, P. (2000). Temporal logics for real-time system specification. *ACM Computing Surveys (CSUR),* 32(1):12–42.

Bennett, M.D. and Audsley, N.C. (2001). Predictable and efficient virtual addressing for safety-critical real-time systems. In *Proceedings of 13th Euromicro Conference on Real-Time Systems,* pages 183–190, Delft, Netherlands. Dept. of Comput. Sci., York Univ.

Bernat, G., Colin, A., and Petters, S.M. (2002). WCET analysis of probabilistic hard real-time systems. In *Proceedings of 23rd IEEE Real-Time Systems Symposium,* pages 279–288, Austin, Texas, USA. Dept. of Comput. Sci., York Univ., UK.

Bondavalli, A., Chiaradonna, S., Giandomenico, F. Di, and Grandoni, F. (1997). Discriminating fault rate and persistency to improve fault treatment. In *Proceedings of The Twenty-Seventh Annual International Symposium on Fault-Tolerant Computing (FTCS'97),* pages 354–362. IEEE.

Bosch (1991). *CAN Specification, Version 2.0.* Robert Bosch Gmbh, Stuttgart, Germany.

Bosch (1998). Robert Bosch GmBH. Fahrsicherheitssysteme. 2. Auflage. Braunschweig/Wiesbaden.

Bretz, E. (2001). By-wire cars turn the corner. *IEEE Spectrum,* 38(4):68–73.

Brodie, M.L. and Stonebreaker, M. (1995). *Migrating legacy systems.* Morgan Kaufmann.

Burns, A. (1993). Scheduling distributed safety critical systems. *IEE Colloquium on Safety Critical Distributed Systems.* Dept. of Comput. Sci., York Univ., Heslington, London, UK.

Busi, N. and Zavattaro, G. (2001). Publish/subscribe vs. shared dataspace coordination infrastructures. In *Proceedings of 10th IEEE International Workshops on Enabling Technologies: Infrastructure for Collaborative Enterprises,* pages 328–333. Dept. of Comput. Sci., Bologna Univ.

Butler, R.W., J.L. Caldwell, and Vito, B.L. Di (1991). Design strategy for a formally verified reliable computing platform. In *Proceedings of the 6th Annual Conference on Computer Assurance (COMPASS), Systems Integrity, Software Safety and Process Security,* pages 125–133, Gaithersburg, MD, USA. NASA Langley Res. Center.

CAN in Automation (1996). *CANopen Communication Profile for Industrial Systems, Draft Standard 301.* CAN in Automation (CiA).

CAN in Automation (2003). *CAN controller chips.* CAN in Automation (CiA). www.can-cia.de/products/can/chips/.

Carter, W.C. (1982). A time for reflection. In *Proceedings of the 8th IEEE International Symposium on Fault tolerand Computing (FTCS-8),* page 41, Santa Monica.

Carzaniga, A., Rosenblum, D.S., and Wolf, A.L. (1999). Interfaces and algorithms for a wide-area event notification service. Technical Report CU-CS-888-99, Department of Computer Science, University of Colorado.

Cervin, A. (2000). *The Real-Time Control Systems Simulator. Reference Manual.* Department of Automatic Control Lund Institute of Technology.

Chandra, T.D., Hadzilacos, V., and Toueg, S. (1996). The weakest failure detector for solving consensus. *Journal of the ACM (JACM),* 43(4):685–722.

Chandra, T.D. and Toueg, S. (1996). Unreliable failure detectors for reliable distributed systems. *Journal of the ACM (JACM)*, 43(2):225–267.

Chandra, U. and Harmon, M.G. (1995). Predictability of program execution times on superscalar pipelined architectures. In *Proceedings of the Third Workshop on Parallel and Distributed Real-Time Systems*, pages 104–112, Santa Barbara, CA, USA. Dept. of Comput. & Inf. Syst, Florida A&M Univ., Tallahassee, FL.

Chang, J.-M. and Maxemchuk, N.F. (1984). Reliable broadcast protocols. *ACM Transactions on Computer Systems (TOCS)*, 2(3):251–273.

Chung, T.M. and Dietz, H.G. (1996). Static scheduling of hard real-time code with instruction-level timing accuracy. In *Proceedings of Third International Workshop on Real-Time Computing Systems and Applications*, pages 203–211, Seoul, South Korea. Sung Kyun Kwan Univ., Suwon.

Collinson, R. (1999). Fly-by-wire flight control. *Computing & Control Engineering Journal*, 10:141–152.

Coulouris, G., Dollimore, J., and Kindberg, T. (1994). *Distributed Systems: Concepts and Design*. International Computer Science Series, Addison-Wesley, second edition.

Cristian, F. (1991a). Reaching agreement on processor-group membership in synchronous distributed systems. *Distributed Computing*, 4:175–187.

Cristian, F. (1991b). Understanding fault-tolerant distributed systems. *Communications of the ACM*, 34(2):56–78.

Cristian, F., Aghali, H., Strong, R., and Dolev, D. (1985). Atomic broadcast: From simple message diffusion to byzantine agreement. In *Proceedings of 15th International Symposium on Fault-Tolerant Computing (FTCS-15)*, pages 200–206, Ann Arbor, MI, USA. IEEE Computer Society Press.

Cristian, F. and Fetzer, C. (1999). The timed asynchronous distributed system model. *IEEE Transactions on Parallel and Distributed Systems*, 10. San Diego, La Jolla, CA, Dept. of Comput. Sci., California Univ.

Deering, S. and Hinden, R. (1998). RFC 2460: Internet protocol, version 6 (IPv6) specification. The Internet Engineering Task Force, www.ietf.org/rfc.html.

Deicke, A. (2002). The electrical/electronic diagnostic concept of the new 7 series. In *Proceedings of Convergence International Congress & Exposition On Transportation Electronics*, Detroit, MI, USA. SAE.

DeLine, R. (1999). *Resolving Packaging Mismatch*. PhD thesis, Carnegie Mellon University, Computer Science Department, Pittsburgh.

Dolev, D., Dwork, C., and Stockmeyer, L. (1987). On the minimal synchronism needed for distributed consensus. *Journal of the ACM (JACM)*, 34(1):77–97.

Edwards, S., Lavagno, L., Lee, E.A., and Sangiovanni-Vincentelli, A. (1997). Design of embedded systems: Formal models, validation, and synthesis. *Proceedings of the IEEE*.

Engblom, J. (2003). Analysis of the execution time unpredictability caused by dynamic branch prediction. In *Proceedings of the 9th IEEE Real-Time and Embedded Technology and Applications Symposium*, pages 152–159, Toronto, Canada. Uppsala University.

Fischer, M.J. (1983). The consensus problem in unreliable distributed systems (a brief survey). *Fundamentals of Computation Theory*, pages 127–140.

Fischer, M.J., Lynch, N.A., and Paterson, M.S. (1985). Impossibility of distributed consensus with one faulty process. *Journal of the ACM (JACM)*, 32(2):374–382.

Fredriksson, L. (1995). A CAN kingdom. Technical report, KVASER AB, Sweden.

Ghezzi, C. and Vigna, G. (1997). Mobile code paradigms and technologies: A case study. In *Proceedings of the First International Workshop on Mobile Agents*, Berlin, Germany.

Godavarty, S., Broyles, S., and Parten, M. (2000). Interfacing to the on-board diagnostic system. In *Proceedings of 52nd IEEE Vehicular Technology Conference*, pages 2000–2004, Boston, MA, USA. Dept. of Electr. Eng., Texas Tech. Univ., Lubbock, TX.

Goldwasser, S., Micali, S., and Rivest, R. L. (1988). A digital signature scheme secure against adaptive chosen-message attacks. *SIAM Journal of Computing,* pages 281–308.

Guerraoui, R. and Schiper, A. (1997). Consensus: the big misunderstanding [distributed fault tolerant systems]. In *Proceedings of the Sixth IEEE Computer Society Workshop on Future Trends of Distributed Computing Systems,* pages 183–188.

Hansen Report (2002). The Hansen Report on Automotive Electronics. Portsmouth NH USA, www. hansenreport.com.

Hansson, H., Lawson, H., Bridal, O., Eriksson, C., Larsson, S., Lön, H., and Strömberg, M. (1997). BASEMENT: An architecture and methodology for distributed automotive real-time systems. *IEEE Transactions on Computers,* 46(9): 1016–1027.

Hansson, H. and Sjödin, M. (1995). An off-line scheduler and system simulator for the BASEMENT distributed real-time system. In *Proceedings of 20th IFAC/IFIP Workshop on Real-Time Programming.*

Harrison, T.H., Levine, D.L., and Schmidt, D.C. (1997). The design and performance of a real-time CORBA event service. In *Proceedings of the ACM Conference on Object-Oriented Programming, Systems, Languages, and Applications,* pages 184–200. ACM Press.

Hayhurst, K., Dorsey, C., Knight, J., Leveson, N., and McCormick, G. (1999). Streamlining software aspects of certification: Report on the SSAC survey. Technical report, NASA Technical Memorandum 1999-209519.

Heiner, G. and Thurner, T. (1998). Time-triggered architecture for safety-related distributed real-time systems in transportation systems. In *Proceedings of the Twenty-Eighth Annual International Symposium on Fault-Tolerant Computing,* pages 402–407.

Henriksson, D., Cervin, A., and Arzen, K.E. (2002). TrueTime: simulation of control loops under shared computer resources. In *Proceedings of the 15th IFAC World Congress on Automatic Control,* Barcelona, Spain. Department of Automatic Control, Lund Institute of Technology.

Hoyme, K. and Driscoll, K. (1993). SAFEbus. *IEEE Aerospace and Electronic Systems Magazine,* 8:34–39.

Hu, X.S., Zhou, T., and Sha, E.H.-M. (2001). Estimating probabilistic timing performance for real-time embedded systems. *IEEE Transactions on Very Large Scale Integration (VLSI) Systems, Special Issue on System Level Design,* 9:833–845.

Intel Corporation (1995). *82527 Serial Communications Controller, Controller Area Network Protocol.* Intel Corporation.

International Standardization Organisation (1994). *Open System Interconnection Model.* International Standardization Organisation, ISO 7498.

Iren, S., Amer, P.D., and Conrad, P.T. (1999). The transport layer: tutorial and survey. *ACM Computing Surveys (CSUR),* 31(4):360–404.

Isermann, R., Schwarz, R., and Stolzl, S. (2002). Fault-tolerant drive-by-wire systems. *IEEE Control Systems Magazine,* 22:64–81.

Johannsen, W., Lamersdorf, W., and Reinhardt, K. (1988). Architecture and design of an open systems LAN/WAN gateway. In *Proceedings of the Computer Networking Symposium,* pages 112–119. IEEE.

Johnson, S.C. and Butler, R.W. (1992). Design for validation. *IEEE Aerospace and Electronic Systems Magazine,* 7(1):38–43.

Jones, C., Kopetz, H., Powell, D., Gaudel, M.-C., Issarny, V., Marsden, E., Moffat, N., Paulitsch, M., Randell, B., Romanovsky, A., Stroud, R., and Taiani, F. (2002). Final version of the DSoS conceptual model. *DSoS Project (IST-1999-11585) Deliverable CSDA1.* Available as Research Report 54/2002 at http://www.vmars.tuwien.ac.at.

Kaiser, J. and Livani, M.A. (1999). Achieving fault-tolerant ordered broadcasts in CAN. In *Proceedings of European Dependable Computing Conference,* pages 351–363.

Karn, P. and Partridge, C. (1988). Improving round-trip time estimates in reliable transport protocols. In *Proceedings of the ACM Workshop on Frontiers in Computer Communications Technology*, pages 2–7. ACM Press.

Kelly, T. (1999). *Arguing Safety – A systematic approach to managing safety cases*. PhD thesis, University of York.

Kieckhafer, R.M., Walter, C.J., Finn, A.M., and Thambidurai, P.M. (1988). The MAFT architecture for distributed fault tolerance. *IEEE Transactions on Computers*, 37:398–404.

Koch, T. and Murer, S. (1999). Service architecture integrated mainframes in a CORBA environment. In *Proceedings of 3rd International Enterprise Distributed Object Computing Conference*, pages 194–203, Mannheim, Germany.

Kopetz, H. (1992). Sparse time versus dense time in distributed real-time systems. In *Proceedings of 12th International Conference on Distributed Computing Systems*, Japan.

Kopetz, H. (1993). Should responsive systems be event-triggered or time-triggered? *Transactions on Information and Systems*, pages pp. E76–D(11):1325–1332.

Kopetz, H. (1995a). Fundamental conflicts in the design of real-time protocols. In *Proceedings of the 2nd International Workshop on Real-Time Computing Systems and Applications*, page 132.

Kopetz, H. (1995b). Why time-triggered architectures will succeed in large hard real-time systems. In *Proceedings of the 5th IEEE Computer Society Workshop on Future Trends of Distributed Computing Systems*, Cheju Island, Korea.

Kopetz, H. (1997). *Real-Time Systems, Design Principles for Distributed Embedded Applications*. Kluwer Academic Publishers, Boston, Dordrecht, London.

Kopetz, H. (1998a). Component-based design of large distributed real-time systems. *Control Engineering Practic – A Journal of IFAC*, 6:53–60. Pergamon Press.

Kopetz, H. (1998b). The time–triggered model of computation. In *Proceedings of the 19th IEEE Real-Time Systems Symposium*, pages 168–177.

Kopetz, H. (1999a). Elementary versus composite interfaces in distributed real-time systems. In *Proceedings of the International Symposium on Autonomous Decentralized Systems*, Tokyo, Japan.

Kopetz, H. (1999b). *Specification of the TTP/C Protocol*. TTTech, Schönbrunner Straße 7, A-1040 Vienna. Available at http://www.ttpforum.org.

Kopetz, H. (2001). The temporal specification of interfaces in distributed real-time systems. In *Proceedings of the EMSOFT 2001*, pages 223–236, Tahoe City, California, USA.

Kopetz, H. (2003). Fault containment and error detection in the time-triggered architecture. In *Proceedings of the Sixth International Symposium on Autonomous Decentralized Systems*.

Kopetz, H. and Bauer, G. (2003). The time-triggered architecture. *IEEE Special Issue on Modeling and Design of Embedded Software*.

Kopetz, H. and Grünsteidl, G. (1994). TTP– a protocol for fault-tolerant real-time systems. *Computer*, 27(1):14–23. Vienna University of Technology, Real-Time Systems Group.

Kopetz, H., Grünsteidl, G., and Reisinger, J. (1991). Fault-tolerant membership service in a synchronous distributed real-time system. *Dependable Computing for Critical Applications (A. Avizienis and J. C. Laprie, Eds.), pp.411-29, Springer-Verlag, Wien, Austria*.

Kopetz, H. and Kim, K. H. (1990). Temporal uncertainties in interactions among real-time objects. In *Proceedings of Ninth Symposium on Reliable Distributed Systems*, pages 165–174, Huntsville, AL , USA. Inst. fuer Tech. Inf., Tech. Univ. of Vienna.

Kopetz, H. and Nossal, R. (1995). The cluster compiler – a tool for the design of time-triggered real-time systems. In *Proceedings of the ACM SIGPLAN 1995 Workshop on Languages, Compilers, & Tools for Real-Time Systems*, pages 108–116. ACM Press.

Kopetz, H. and Nossal, R. (1997). Temporal firewalls in large distributed realtime systems. In *Proceedings of IEEE Workshop on Future Trends in Distributed Computing*, Tunis, Tunesia. IEEE Press.

Kopetz, H. and Obermaisser, R. (2002). Temporal composability. *Computing & Control Engineering Journal,* 13:156–162.

Kopetz, H. and Ochsenreiter, W. (1987). Clock synchronization in distributed real time systems. *IEEE Transactions on Computers.*

Kopetz, H. and Reisinger, J. (1993). The non-blocking write protocol NBW: A solution to a real-time synchronisation problem. In *Proceedings of the 14th Real-Time Systems Symposium, Raleigh-Durham, North Carolina, USA.*

Kopetz, H. and Suri, N. (2003). Compositional design of RT systems: A conceptual basis for specification of linking interfaces. In *Proceedings of Sixth IEEE International Symposium on Object-Oriented Real-Time Distributed Computing,* pages 51–60.

Lala, J.H. and Harper, R.E. (1994). Architectural principles for safety-critical real-time applications. *Proceedings of the IEEE,* 82:25–40.

Lamport, L. (1984). Using time instead of timeouts for fault-tolerant distributed systems. *ACM Trans. on Programming Languages and Systems,* pages 254–280.

Lamport, L., Shostak, R., and Pease, M. (1982). The byzantine generals problem. *ACM Transactions on Programming Languages and Systems (TOPLAS),* 4(3):382–401.

Laprie, J.C. (1992). *Dependability: Basic Concepts and Terminology.* Springer Verlag, Vienna, Austria.

Larrea, M., Fernández, A., and Arévalo, S. (2000). Optimal implementation of the weakest failure detector for solving consensus (brief announcement). In *Proceedings of the 19th Annual ACM Symposium on Principles of Distributed Computing,* page 334. ACM Press.

Lawrenz, W. (1995). Worldwide status of CAN - present and future. In *Proceedings of 2nd international CAN Conference,* pages 0–12, London.

Lee, P.A. and Anderson, T. (1990). *Fault Tolerance Principles and Practice,* volume 3 of *Dependable Computing and Fault-Tolerant Systems.* Springer Verlag.

Leen, G. and Heffernan, D. (2002). Expanding automotive electronic systems. *Computer,* 35(1):88–93.

Leen, G., Heffernan, D., and Dunne, A. (1999). Digital networks in the automotive vehicle. *Computing & Control Engineering Journal,* 10:257–266. Dept. of Electron. & Control Eng., Limerick Univ.

Lehoczky, J.P. (1996). Real-time queueing theory. In *Proceedings of 17th IEEE Real-Time Systems Symposium,* pages 186–195.

Livani, M.A. (1999). SHARE: A transparent approach to fault-tolerant broadcast in CAN. In *Proceedings of 6th International CAN Conference (ICC6),* Torino, Italy.

Lowery, H., Mitchell, B., Stewart, D., and Tran, T. (2001). Feasibility of modernizing F-15 avionics using an open systems approach. In *Proceedings of the 20th Conference on Digital Avionics Systems,* volume 2, pages 9A2/1–9A2/7.

Lundelius, J. and Lynch, N. (1984). A new fault-tolerant algorithm for clock synchronization. In *Proceedings of the Third Annual ACM Symposium on Principles of Distributed Computing,* pages 75–88. ACM Press.

Lundelius-Welch, J. and Lynch, N. A. (1984). An upper and lower bound for clock synchronization. *Information and Control,* 62:190–204.

Lynch, N. (1989). A hundred impossibility proofs for distributed computing. In *Proceedings of the eighth annual ACM Symposium on Principles of distributed computing,* pages 1–28. ACM Press.

Maffeis, S. (1998). Client/server term definition. In Hemmendinger, D., Ralston, A., and Reilly, E. D., editors, *Encyclopedia of Computer Science.* International Thomson Computer Publishing.

Mantegazza, P., Bianchi, E., Dozio, L., Angelo, M., and Beal, D. (2000). *RTAI Programming Guide.* Dipartimento di Ingegneria Aerospaziale Politecnico di Milano (DIAPM).

McKinney, J.M. (1969). A survey of analytical time-sharing models. *ACM Computing Surveys (CSUR),* 1(2):105–116.

Mesarovic, M.D. and Takahara, Y. (1989). *Abstract Systems Theory, chapter 3.* Springer-Verlag.

Morris, J., Lee, G., Parker, K., Bundell, G.A., and Chiou, P.L. (2001). Software component certification. *Computer,* 34(9):30–36.

MOST Cooperation (2002). *MOST Specification Version 2.2.* MOST Cooperation, Karlsruhe, Germany, www.mostnet.de/.

Motorola (2001). *MPC855T User's Manual. Integrated Communications Microprocessor.* Motorola.

Nahum, E., Ramamritham, K., and Stankovic, J. (1992). Real-time interprocess communication in the spring kernel. Technical report, Real-Time & Database Systems Laboratories, Department of Computer Science, University of Massachusetts, Amherst.

Nance, R.E. (1981). The time and state relationships in simulation modeling. *Communications of the ACM,* 24(4):173–179.

NextTTA (2003). NextTTA IST-2001-32111. High Confidence Architecture for Distributed Control Applications, project deliverable D2.4. Emulation of CAN and TCP/IP.

Nicholson, M., Conmy, P., Bate, I., and McDermid, J. (2000). Generating and maintaining a safety argument for integrated modular systems. In *Proceedings of 5th Australian Workshop on Safety Critical Systems and Software,* pages 31–41.

Nolte, T., Hansson, H., and Norstrom, C. (2002). Minimizing CAN response-time jitter by message manipulation. In *Proceedings of Eighth IEEE Symposium on Real-Time and Embedded Technology and Applications,* pages 197–206. Dept. of Comput. Eng., Malardalen Univ., Vasteras.

Noonen, D., Siegel, S., and Maloney, P. (1994). DeviceNet application protocol. In *Proceedings of the 1st International CAN Conference,* Mainz, Germany.

Obermaisser, R. (2003a). CAN emulation prototype implementation. Research Report 47/2003, Technische Universität Wien, Institut für Technische Informatik, Treitlstr. 1-3/182-1, 1040 Vienna, Austria.

Obermaisser, R. (2003b). *An Integrated Architecture for Event-Triggered And Time-Triggered Control Paradigms.* PhD thesis, Technische Universität Wien, Institut für Technische Informatik, Vienna, Austria.

Obermaisser, R. (2004a). CAN emulation in the Time-Triggered Architecture: Validation report. Research Report 12/2004, Technische Universität Wien, Institut für Technische Informatik, Treitlstr. 1-3/182-1, 1040 Vienna, Austria.

Obermaisser, R. (2004b). Protocol emulation algorithm for CAN in the Time-Triggered Architecture. Research Report 25/2004, Technische Universität Wien, Institut für Technische Informatik, Treitlstr. 1-3/182-1, 1040 Vienna, Austria.

OMG (2002a). *Common Object Request Broker Architecture: Core Specification, Version 3.0.2.* Object Management Group (OMG).

OMG (2002b). *CORBA Services Specifications – Notification Service, Version 1.0.1.* Object Management Group (OMG).

Pauli, B., Meyna, A., and Heitmann, P. (1998). Reliability of electronic components and control units in motor vehicle applications. *VDI-Reports 1415.*

Pease, M., Shostak, R., and Lamport, L. (1980). Reaching agreement in the presence of faults. *Journal of the ACM (JACM),* 27(2):228–234.

Pfeifer, H., Schwier, D., and F.W. von Henke (1999). Formal verification for time-triggered clock synchronization. In *Proceedings of 7th IFIP Working Conference on Dependable Computing for Critical Applications,* pages 207–226, San Jose, CA, USA. Fakultat fur Inf., Ulm Univ.

Philips Semiconductors (2000). *SJA1000 Stand-alone CAN controller Product Specification.* Philips Semiconductors, Eindhoven, www-us.semiconductors.philips.com/pip/SJA1000.html.

Pires, L.F., Sinderen, M., and Vissers, C.A. (1993). Advanced design concepts for open distributed systems development. In *Proceedings of the Fourth Workshop on Future Trends of Distributed Computing Systems.*

Poledna, S. (1995). *Fault-Tolerant Real-Time Systems: The Problem of Replica Determinism.* Kluwer Academic Publishers.

Powell, D. (1992). Failure mode assumptions and assumption coverage. In *Proceedings of the 22nd IEEE Annual International Symposium on Fault-Tolerant Computing (FTCS-22)*, pages 386–395, Boston, USA.

Punnekkat, S., Hansson, H., and Norström, C. (2000). Response time analysis under errors for CAN. In *Proceedings of 6th IEEE Real-Time Technology and Applications Symposium*, pages 258–265.

R. Mores, G. Hay, R. Belschner, J. Berwanger, C. Ebner, S. Fluhrer, E. Fuchs, B. Hedenetz, W. Kuffner, A. Krüger, D. Millinger, P. Lohrmann, M. Peller, J. Ruh, A. Schedl, and M. Sprachmann (March 2001). FlexRay – the communication system for advanced automotive control systems. *SAE 2001 World Congress, Detroit, MI, USA*, Doc.No 2001-01-0676.

Ran, A. and Xu, J. (1997). Architecting software with interface objects. In *Proceedings of the 8th Israeli Conference on Computer Systems and Software Engineering*, pages 30–37, Herzliya, Israel. Software Technol. Lab., Nokia Res. Center, Espoo.

Randell, B., Lee, P., and Treleaven, P. C. (1978). Reliability issues in computing system design. *ACM Computing Surveys*, 10(2):123–165.

Regehr, J.D. (2001). *Using Hierarchical Scheduling to Support Soft Real-Time Applications in General-Purpose Operating Systems*. PhD thesis, School of Engineering and Applied Science, University of Virginia.

Rostamzadeh, B., Lonn, H., Snedsbol, R., and Torin, J. (1995). DACAPO: a distributed computer architecture for safety-critical control applications. In *Proceedings of the Intelligent Vehicles '95 Symposium*, pages 376–381, Detroit, MI, USA.

RTCA (1992). *DO-178B: Software Considerations in Airborne Systems and Equipment Certification*. Radio Technical Commission for Aeronautics, Inc. (RTCA), Washington, DC.

Rufino, J. (1997). Dual-media redundancy mechanisms for CAN. Technical Report CSTC RT-97-01, Centre de Sistemas Telemáticos e Computacionais do Instituto Superior Técnico, Lisboa, Portugal.

Rufino, J. and Verissimo, P. (1995). A study on the inaccessibility characteristics of the controller area network. In *2nd International CAN Conference*, London, United Kingdom.

Rufino, J., Verissimo, P., Arroz, G., Almeida, C., and Rodrigues, L. (1998). Fault-tolerant broadcasts in CAN. In *Proceedings of the 28th International Symposium on Fault-Tolerant Computing Systems*, pages 150–159, Munich, Germany.

Rushby, J. (1999a). Partitioning for avionics architectures: Requirements, mechanisms, and assurance. NASA Contractor Report CR-1999-209347, NASA Langley Research Center. Also to be issued by the FAA.

Rushby, J. (1999b). Systematic formal verification for fault-tolerant time-triggered algorithms. *IEEE Transactions on Software Engineering*, 25(5):651–660.

Rushby, J. (2001a). Bus architectures for safety-critical embedded systems. In Henzinger, Tom and Kirsch, Christoph, editors, *Proceedings of the First Workshop on Embedded Software (EMSOFT 2001)*, volume 2211 of *Lecture Notes in Computer Science*, pages 306–323, Lake Tahoe, CA. Springer-Verlag.

Rushby, J. (2001b). A comparison of bus architectures for safety-critical embedded systems. Technical report, Computer Science Laboratory, SRI International, Menlo Park, CA. Available at http://www.csl.sri.com/~rushby/abstracts/buscompare.

Rushby, J. (2001c). Modular certification. Technical report, Computer Science Laboratory SRI International, 333 Ravenswood Avenue, Menlo Park, CA 94025, USA.

Sangiovanni-Vincentelli, A. (2002). Defining platform-based design. *EEDesign of EETimes*.

Schneider, F.B. (1993). What good are models and what models are good? *Distributed systems (2nd Ed.), ACM Press/Addison-Wesley Publishing Co.*, pages 17–26.

Segarra, M., Losert, T., and Obermaisser, R. (2003). Hard real-time CORBA: TTP transport definition. Technical Report IST37652/067, Universidad Politecnica de Madrid, Lunds Tekniska Högskola, Technische Universität Wien, SCILabs Ingenieros.

Sinha, A. (1992). Client-server computing. *Communications of the ACM*, 35(7):77–98.

Srikanth, T.K. and Toueg, S. (1987). Optimal clock synchronization. *Journal of the ACM (JACM),* 34(3):626–645.

Stankovic, J.A. (1990). The Spring architecture. In *Proceedings of Euromicro '90 Workshop on Real Time,* pages 104–113, Horsholm, Denmark.

Stankovic, J.A. and Ramamritham, K. (1989). The Spring kernel: a new paradigm for real-time operating systems. *ACM SIGOPS Operating Systems Review,* 23(3):54–71.

Suri, N., Walter, C.J., and Hugue, M.M. (1995). *Advances In Ultra-Dependable Distributed Systems,* chapter 1. IEEE Computer Society Press, 10662 Los Vaqueros Circle, P.O. Box 3014, Los Alamitos, CA 90720-1264.

Swanson, D.L. (1998). Evolving avionics systems from federated to distributed architectures. In *Proceedings of the 17th AIAA/IEEE/SAE Digital Avionics Systems Conference,* pages D26/1– D26/8, Bellevue, WA, USA.

Swingler, J. and McBride, J.W. (1999). The degradation of road tested automotive connectors. In *Proceedings of the 45th IEEE Holm Conference on Electrical Contacts,* pages 146–152, Pittsburgh, PA, USA. Dept. of Mech. Eng., Southampton Univ.

Teal, C. and Sorensen, D. (2001). Condition based maintenance [aircraft wiring]. In *Proceedings of the 20th Conference on Digital Avionics Systems, DASC,* volume 1, pages 3B2/1–3B2/7.

Temple, C. (1998). Avoiding the babbling-idiot failure in a time-triggered communication system. In *Proceedings of the Symposium on Fault-Tolerant Computing,* pages 218–227.

Teo, M. (1995). Real-time multicasting for group communication in the spring kernel. Technical report, Real-Time & Database Systems Laboratories, Department of Computer Science, University of Massachusetts, Amherst.

Thomas, D.A., Ayers, K., and Pecht, M. (2002). The 'trouble not identified' phenomenon in automotive electronics. *Microelectronics Reliability,* 42:641–651.

Tindell, K.W. and Burns, A. (1994). Guaranteed message latencies for distributed safety-critical hard real-time control networks. Technical Report YCS229, Dept. of Computer Science, University of York.

Treleaven, P.C. and Hopkins, R.P. (1981). Decentralized computation. In *Proceedings of the 8th annual symposium on Computer Architecture,* pages 279–290. IEEE Computer Society Press.

TTTech (2002a). *TTP Monitoring Node – A TTP Development Board for the Time-Triggered Architecture.* TTTech Computertechnik AG, Schönbrunner Strasse 7, A-1040 Vienna, Austria.

TTTech (2002b). *TTP/C Controller C2 – Controller Schedule (MEDL) Structure Document.* TTTech Computertechnik AG, Schönbrunner Strasse 7, A-1040 Vienna, Austria.

Veen, A.H. (1986). Dataflow machine architecture. *ACM Computing Surveys (CSUR),* 18(4):365–396.

Verissimo, P. (1997). On the role of time in distributed systems. In *Proceedings of the Sixth IEEE Computer Society Workshop on Future Trends of Distributed Computing Systems,* pages 316–321. IEEE.

Verissimo, P. and Almeida, C. (1995). Quasi-synchronism: a step away from the traditional fault-tolerant real-time system models. *Bulletin of the Technical Committee on Operating Systems and Application Environments (TCOS),* 7(4):35–39.

Verissimo, P. and Marques, J. A. (1990). Reliable broadcast for fault-tolerance on local computer networks. In *Proceedings of the Ninth Symposium on Reliable Distributed Systems,* Huntsville, Alabama-USA.

Verissimo, P., Rufino, J., and Ming, L. (1997). How hard is hard real-time communication on field-buses? In *Proceedings of Symposium on Fault-Tolerant Computing,* pages 112–121.

Verissimo, P., Rufino, J., and Rodrigues, L. (September 1991). Enforcing real-time behaviour of LAN-based protocols. In Proceedings of the 10th IFAC Workshop on Distributed Computer Control Systems, Semmering, Austria, IFAC.

Wallace, L.E. (1994). *Airborne Trailblazer.* National Aeronautics and Space Administration, NASA History Office, Washington, D.C.

Wetzer, J.M., Cliteur, G.J., Rutgers, W.R., and Verhaart, H.F.A. (2000). Diagnostic- and condition assessment-techniques for condition based maintenance. In *Proceedings of the 2000 Annual Report Conference on Electrical Insulation and Dielectric Phenomena,* volume 1, pages 47–51.

Whitrow, G.J. (1990). *The Natural Philosophy of Time.* Oxford Univeristy Press, 2nd edition.

Younis, M., Aboutabl, M., and Kim, D. (2000). An approach for supporting temporal partitioning and software reuse in integrated modular avionics. In *Proceedings of 6th IEEE Real-Time Technology and Applications Symposium,* pages 56–66, Washington, DC, USA. Adv. Syst. Technol. Group, Honeywell Int. Inc., Columbia, MD.

Index